proclamation 2

Aids for Interpreting the Lessons of the Church Year

advent christmas

Frederick Houk Borsch
and
Davie Napier

series a

editors: Elizabeth Achtemeier · Gerhard Krodel · Charles P. Price

FORTRESS PRESS   PHILADELPHIA

Library of Congress Cataloging in Publication Data (Revised)

Main entry under title:

Proclamation 2.

Consists of 24 volumes in 3 series designated A, B, and C which correspond to the cycles of the three year lectionary plus 4 volumes covering the lesser festivals. Each series contains 8 basic volumes with the following titles: Advent-Christmas, Epiphany, Lent, Holy Week, Easter, Pentecost 1, Pentecost 2, and Pentecost 3.
    CONTENTS: [etc.]—Series C: [1] Fuller, R. H. Advent-Christmas. [2] Pervo, R. I. and Carl III, W. J. Epiphany.—Thulin, R. L. et. al. The lesser festivals. 4 v.
    1. Bible—Homiletical use. 2. Bible—Liturgical lessons, English.
[BS534.5.P76]   251   79-7377
ISBN 0-8006-4079-9 (ser. C, v. 1)

8269C80   Printed in the United States of America   1-4091

Contents

Editor's Foreword

This volume of Proclamation 2 deals with the beginning of the church year: Advent and Christmas. It treats the lessons provided in cycle A of the common lectionary.

Christmas is a Christian celebration at the winter solstice. The significance of the date is theological rather than historical. There is no evidence of any kind regarding the date of Jesus' birth. His nativity began to be celebrated on December 25 in Rome during the early part of the fourth century (A.D. 336) as a Christian counterpart to the pagan festival, popular among worshipers of Mithras, called Sol Invictis, the Unconquerable Sun. At the very moment when the days are the shortest and darkness seems to have conquered light, the sun passes its nadir. Days grow longer, and although the cold will only increase for quite a long time, the ultimate conquest of winter is sure. This astronomical process is a parable of the career of the Incarnate One. At the moment when history is blackest, and in the least expected and obvious place, the Son of God is born. And although his life proceeds from a manger to a cross, and his conflicts only increase, the ultimate conquest of death is sure. William Temple once wrote, "Only if God is revealed in the rising of the sun in the sky can he be revealed in the rising of a son of man from the dead" (*Nature, Man, and God* [New York: Macmillan Co., 1935], p. 306).

Advent is the season of preparation for Christmas. It once extended for five or six weeks beforehand, but since the time of Gregory I (590–608), the season of Advent has been fixed as the four Sundays before Christmas.

The chief themes of Advent are divine judgment and the coming of God's kingdom on one hand, and human repentance and obedience on the other. In cycle A, the first year's cycle of lessons, these themes are articulated through passages from the First Gospel and related First and Second Lessons. On the first Sunday, we are asked to consider God's second coming in glory to judge the living and the dead, through Jesus' announcement of the Son of man, who is to come "as a thief in the night." On the second Sunday, we encounter John the Baptist's preaching of the nearness of the kingdom of heaven, and on

5

the third, Jesus is presented as the fulfiller of the Baptist's expectations. On the Fourth Sunday in Advent, we hear the annunciation to Joseph of the birth of the Savior.

The preacher's task is so to grasp the significance of these ancient events, and of the commentary on them provided in First and Second Lessons, that he or she can be the completely contemporary agent of the same proclamation: "Repent, for the kingdom of heaven is at hand"; "Glory to God in the highest and peace to his people on earth"; "For unto you is born this day in the city of David a Savior."

The exegetical material of this volume has been prepared by the Very Reverend Frederick Houk Borsch, Dean of the Chapel at Princeton University and formerly Dean of the Church Divinity School of the Pacific in Berkeley, California. He is the author of *The Son of Man in Myth and History, The Christian and Gnostic Son of Man,* and *God's Parable.*

Homiletical commentary has been provided by the Reverend Davie Napier, Master of Calhoun College at Yale University and professor of Old Testament at Yale Divinity School. He is the former president of the Pacific School of Religion and former Dean of the Chapel of Stanford University. His published works include *Song of the Vineyard; Come, Sweet Death; On New Creation;* and *Word of God, Word of Earth.*

Alexandria, Va.   CHARLES P. PRICE

The First Sunday in Advent

Lutheran	Roman Catholic	Episcopal	Pres/UCC/Chr	Meth/COCU
Isa. 2:1–5	Isa. 2:1–5	Isa. 2:1–5	Isa. 2:1–5	Isa. 2:1–5
Rom. 13:11–14	Rom. 13:11–14	Rom. 13:8–14	Rom. 13:11–14	Rom. 13:8–14
Matt. 24:37–44 or Matt. 21:1–11	Matt. 24:37–44	Matt. 24:37–44	Matt. 24:36–44	Matt. 24:36–44

EXEGESIS

First Lesson: Isa. 2:1–5. The opening verse closely parallels the introduction to the entire book (1:1) and appears to serve as a heading for a collection of prophecies of warning and promise which comprise chaps. 2—4 (or 2—5). We are thus meant to understand that these oracles come from approximately the second half of the eighth century B.C. This was a time of considerable internal turmoil and political intrigue when there were severe threats against both Judah and Israel by foreign powers. Some scholars contend, however, that the prophecy contained in vv. 2–4 may belong to the time of Second Isaiah, two centuries later, when the Exile was drawing to a close.

The whole first chapter of Isaiah is an arraignment against Judah since it has rejected the Lord as its true sovereign and worshiped false gods. But there are also words of hope, if Israel will make a new beginning. In the manner of many of the prophetic books of the OT, warnings and denunciations are followed by visions of a new possibility after repentance. Our passage, at the beginning of the second chapter, is one such *vision.* It is a *word* received from God through the prophet; that is, it is meant to be understood as a divinely inspired revelation.

"The days to come" or "the latter days" (v. 2) refer to Judah's new age, pointing beyond this period of troubled history to the time of the culmination of God's promises. Then the mountain of the Lord's house (Mount Zion) will figuratively become the highest, most exalted mountain on earth, the holiest of places. It becomes, as it were, the successor to Mount Sinai as the place where the Lord reveals the truth for humankind. As a result, peoples from the world over will flow like water toward Zion, coming to recognize that the word of the Lord's prophet and the instruction of the law offer the true way and path for all peoples. The passage thus depicts a form of universalism (all nations coming to know and obey Yahweh's rule) which will be elaborated upon at later points in the OT and NT.

This time of great revelation, it must be remembered, is the work of the Lord, but because of the people's obedient response, God will become the judge of all—not to accuse as in the earlier prophecies of gloom, but to enable a universal peace among nations. The instruments of war will be transformed into the tools of agriculture. Arms and armies will no longer be needed.

V. 5 is a closing admonition and a bridge to the next oracle. All Israel is to seek the new vision by walking in the light of the Lord (a familiar image for observing the teaching in the presence of the Lord).

Second Lesson: Rom. 13:8-14. This letter is addressed to a relatively new group of Christians whom Paul has not yet met but plans soon to visit. He has previously set forth his understanding of how both Jews (with the law of Moses) and Gentiles (without it) are sinners before God but now can find God's gracious acceptance and a new right relationship through faith because of what God has accomplished in Jesus. The concluding portions of the epistle (chaps. 12—15) offer instruction and exhortation concerning the new manner of life for believers.

Christians have many specific responsibilities (13:1-7 discuss those toward the state), but the ultimate and essential "obligation" is a love for one's neighbor. This commandment is seen as the highest expression of the law with regard to one's concern for others (Lev. 19:18). It was also emphasized by Jewish teachers of the time and given prominent place in the recollection of Jesus' own words (Mark 12:31). Paul repeats the theme in Gal. 5:14 (see 1 Thess. 4:9), and it continues to be a central motif for all Christian ethics (cf. James 2:18; 1 Pet. 1:22).

Paul's attitude toward the law was both complex and profound: "Christ is the *end* of the law" (Rom. 10:4 RSV). In the following of Jesus, disciples discover the way which completes and surpasses the intention of every form of legal precept. Trying to help a neighbor without *agape*-love will do no real good, while genuine care for another (as being like oneself) will bring to fulfillment all that God intended in the provision of the law (v. 10). From this perspective, the law, when interpreted by and subject to the love of Christ, remains a useful guide.

Vv. 11-14 may seem like a sudden switch in theme, but they actually provide the context, often stressed by Paul, which makes possible the distinct style of Christian life. The new age first announced by Jesus, has begun. The references to the *hour* and the *kairos* (the time of opportunity) echo Jesus' own words and the thrust of many of his parables. Both Jesus and Paul believed that the final movements of the consummation of human history had already commenced. There was little time left. In one sense they may be thought to have been mistaken. Nevertheless, at a deeper level of human experience, the truth of their message may be realized. There is no time to respond but *now.* This is the only hour in which salvation through the response of faith can take place.

Familiar imagery of waking from sleep and of night passing into day is then used. The language echoes passages from the OT and from sectarian groups of Jesus' time (especially the Qumran community). While the sharp contrast of light and darkness may seem to overlook the nuances of many human moral choices, it is intended to throw the fundamental decision for good over evil into bold relief. This imagery, together with the references to "taking off" and "putting on" and to the avoidance of former evil conduct, is based on a pattern of Christian teaching apparently used in connection with baptism. (Cf. Col. 3:5-17; Eph. 4:25—5:20; 6:10-20.) The armor of light is more fully described in 1 Thess. 5:8 and Eph. 6:11-17. This defense against evil, along with the development in the Christlike life begun at baptism, means that the Christian "puts on" Christ Jesus. He is both the ultimate mode of protection and the pattern toward which disciples grow (Col. 3:10; Eph. 5:1-3) since they have become incorporate into his new life. (Cf. Rom 6:11; Gal. 3:27; Col. 2:6-7.)

Gospel: Matt. 24:37-44. Drawing on sayings from the so-called Q material, Matthew adds to an eschatological discourse which he has otherwise largely taken over from Mark three analogies (vv. 37-41) describing the sudden and unexpected character of the final time. Jesus is here pictured (24:3) teaching his disciples privately while sitting on the Mount of Olives (the mountain just to the east of Jerusalem on which it was traditionally believed the Lord would appear on the Day of Judgment; see Zech. 14:4).

One is cognizant, however, that the evangelist is doing far more than merely recording sayings attributed to Jesus. He is using these little stories to address disciples of his own time who were likely troubled by the disparity between their Lord's words, which seemed to predict a swift ending to human history, and the fact that at least a generation had passed since Jesus' death. The perceptive listener, therefore, hears these sayings both in the setting of Jesus' earthly ministry and in the light of the reflective concern of the later Christian community.

V. 36 reminds the disciples that only the Father knows the day and hour, and the three illustrations regarding the surprising manner in which the end will come then follow. This message stands in considerable contrast to the "program eschatology" found elsewhere in the Gospels (cf., e.g., vv. 4–35 and 2 Thess. 2), which maintains that the end will not take place until certain predictable events have happened. While one can appreciate how both types of proclamation could have had their place in Jesus' teaching and how both can be used to heighten the sense of excitement for those looking for the advent of the kingdom, many scholars believe that the "imminent eschatology" (the end will come suddenly without warning) illustrated by this passage was far more characteristic of Jesus' message.

As no one knew what was about to happen in Noah's time, so will it be in this age. People go about their ordinary, everyday activities. There seems nothing particularly wrong about what they are doing; their problem is that they are not alert and ready. One may surmise that the evangelist was warning against laxness and indifference in his own generation. The end and fulfillment of human history may be delayed but still will come.

The two references to "the coming of the Son of man" in v. 37 and the end of v. 39 neatly frame a little parable. "Coming" (*parousia*) is employed as a kind of technical term in this chapter (vv. 3, 27, 37, 39) and is also used by Paul, and then more widely to refer to the return of Jesus. The background and development in Christian circles of the designation "Son of man" is still far from fully understood. In sayings such as these Jesus may have used it to refer to a heavenly, eschatological judge. Whether or not he associated himself directly with the figure, disciples came to think of Jesus as this Son of man.

Vv. 40–41 present a somewhat different emphasis. No one knows who will be *taken* (the word suggests a gathering of the elect; see v. 30) and who left. Human judgment apparently offers little guidance to help in understanding this form of distinctive separation of the elect and the lost. Nor is there any reference to their moral behavior, though it is probably to be understood that God alone has perceived their true character and perhaps their state of preparedness.

The little parable of the alert householder (vv. 42–44) anticipates the theme found in the subsequent story (vv. 45–51) of the wise and watchful servant, as well as the parables of Matthew 25. The image of the unexpected thief is also used in 1 Thess. 5:2, 4; 2 Pet. 3:10; Rev. 3:3 (and see Gospel of Thomas 21b and 103). The focus here, however, is meant to be on the attitude of the householder, and the message and wording of v. 44 neatly sum up the thrust of the whole passage.

HOMILETICAL INTERPRETATION

Certainly for most of us brought up in the church, the Advent-Christmas season is the tenderest and most poignant time in the church year. As the days grow shorter toward the winter solstice just a few days before Christmas, the face of our faith is warmed and brightened in expectation of that most incredible of all the gifts of God, the gift to the world of the great Liberator of humanity—in the form, first, of a newborn infant, as defenseless and vulnerable and innocent as a lamb!

First Lesson: Isa. 2:1-5. These magnificent lines (vv. 2-4) appear in Mic. 4:1-3 with this added soaring conclusion (v.4):

> All people will live in peace
>   among their own vineyards and fig trees,
>   and no one will make them afraid.

We can understand the fervor and intensity of this "floating" oracle, as some have called it, when we recall that perhaps no single strip of the earth's surface has witnessed greater, more persistent violence than what we have called Palestine, that little corridor about a hundred fifty miles long from north to south, and no more than fifty miles wide at its broadest, caught in the midst of the great powers through all the centuries of recorded history, and familiar with all the forms of human aggression from the most primitive to the most sophisticated weapons.

Is the prophets' vision of that coming day when humankind will "study war no more" intended to be a projection into real history, or is it a cheap utopian shot, devoid of substantial historical human hope? Given the total biblical context, given the irrepressible biblical faith from the call of Abraham to the whole Christ Event, given the promise of the blessing of the families of the earth (five times repeated in the stories of the ancestors: Gen. 12:3; 18:18; 22:18; 26:4; 28:14) and the invasion of the Redeeming Word and the affirmation of human history in the incarnation—given all this, it is difficult to

believe that the prophets would add to their projections of peace and
blessing the cynical line, "We can dream, can't we?"

Second Lesson: Rom. 13:8-14. The juxtaposition of texts before
us is perceptive, although aptness of juxtaposition is not always
characteristic of lectionaries. If we are seriously to address the now
absolutely critical task of conversion of our economy from the mam-
moth and obscene creation of instruments of war to the creation of instruments of peace, shalom, total human well-being; if we are to be
seriously about the business of "Advent," which is the coming of the
Person and realm of peace, we will take Paul's words to this "relatively new group of Christians" (see exegesis) as also addressed to us,
the more so since we propose to become new (renewed) Christians in
this season.

If it is in any meaningful sense to be "swords into plowshares," this
lesson shows us where to begin. "Leave no claim outstanding against
you except that of mutual love. . . . Love cannot wrong a neighbor"
(vv. 8, 10 NEB). We would do well to remind ourselves that the Great
Commandment, on the second part of which Paul is playing, has its
origin among the people of the prophets and the ancient Torah ("instruction") clearly influenced by the prophets. Total and passionate
love of God is first enjoined in Deut. 6:5; and love of neighbor, specifically stated, occurs first in the Bible in Lev. 19:18. It is difficult to
think that Paul, exceptionally well-versed in Scripture, could have
quoted the commandment on love of neighbor in Lev. 19:18 without
having in mind the context of that commandment which, as he says,
sums up all the commandments. When he says, "Let us behave with
decency" (v. 13 NEB), he may be thinking not only of the Ten Commandments, the Decalogue, from which he quotes in v. 9, but as well
the context of "love of neighbor" in Leviticus 19. Indeed it may well
be, as some have suggested, that we have embedded in that chapter
another Decalogue climaxed in this commandment to love our neighbors. If so, it would look like this, and it would add particularity to
Paul's admonition to "behave with decency."

Leviticus 19 RSV (emphasis added):
1. V. 11. You shall not steal, nor deal falsely, nor lie to one another.
2. V. 12. You shall not swear by my name falsely, and so profane the
   name of your God.
3. V. 13a. You shall not oppress your neighbor or rob him. [If we think
   of neighbor in the global sense, as we must, it isn't difficult to trans-

late this into the whole-scale oppression of our day of the poor of the earth by the rich.]

4. V. 13b. The wages of a hired servant shall not remain with you all night until the morning. [Let your homiletical intuition range over this one.]

5. V. 14. You shall not curse the deaf or put a stumbling block before the blind, but you shall fear [honor, glorify] your God.

6. V. 15. You shall do no injustice in judgment; you shall not be partial to the poor or defer to the great, but in righteousness shall you judge your neighbor.

7. V. 16a. You shall not go up and down as a slanderer among your people.

8. V. 16b. You shall not stand forth against the life of your neighbor.

9. V. 17. You shall not hate your brother [sister, contemporary, neighbor in the universal sense] *in your heart,* but you shall reason with your neighbor, lest you bear sin because of [them].

10. V. 18. You shall not take vengeance or bear any grudge against . . . your own people [who, in Christ, are the world of folk for whom he died], but you shall love your neighbor as yourself.

This series of commandments, along with the more familiar Ten Commandments, may well be the context out of which Paul speaks when he calls for a life of "decency," as the New English Bible puts it.

Gospel: Matt. 24:37-44. If the earliest Christian community expected momentarily the return of Christ, the passing of years and even decades brought on a stance of patient expectation. Our Gospel text concludes: "Hold yourselves ready, therefore, because the Son of Man will come at the time you least expect him" (v. 44 NEB). Live your days fully and patiently and always in the awareness of the immediate possible "coming" of Christ. Don't make special preparation. *Live* prepared. *Be* prepared. Fulfill your days always in expectation of the Great Surprise.

Most of us do not look for the "coming" with the literal expectations of the first Christians. We tend to believe that the "coming" always *is,* that indeed we live in the presence of Christ who in every moment freshly invades our present, redeems our past, and gives us hope for the future, however discouraging the immediate prognosis. In the round of the church year, we annually celebrate and reaffirm this unceasing quality of Christ' comingness in the Advent-Christmas sequence of events.

If you already know a little book called *Letters to a Young Poet,* by

Rainer Maria Rilke (New York: W. W. Norton & Co., 1962), you will bless me for quoting from it. If you don't, and these lines persuade you that you must, you will doubly bless me.

In a letter to a young poet written in the fall or winter of 1903, Rilke wrote (pp. 49ff.):

> Why do you not think of Christ as the coming one, imminent from all eternity? . . . what keeps you from projecting his birth into times that are in process of becoming, and living your life like a painful and beautiful day in the history of a great gestation? For do you not see that everything that happens keeps on being a beginning, and could it not be *His* beginning, since beginning is in itself always so beautiful? . . . Be patient and without resentment and think that the least we can do is to make his becoming not more difficult for him than the earth makes it for the spring when it wants to come.

And in November Rilke moved into new surroundings in Rome. On 19 December of that year, he wrote in one of his letters into which characteristically he poured himself and his creative genius (p. 107):

> I am now pretty well installed in the little house. It lacks nothing save that which I cannot give it—save life, which is in all things and in me; save work, which binds one thing to another and links everything with the great necessity; save joy, which comes from within and from activity; save patience, which can wait for what comes from afar.

It is the sense of our texts, taken together, and of the season into which we have come, that we are to live in constant expectation of great surprises which will descend like angels; and that Christ, who always *is*, is also coming afresh, with renewed promise that our ways of darkness and death will be converted to programs and instruments of light and life.

The Second Sunday in Advent

Lutheran	Roman Catholic	Episcopal	Pres/UCC/Chr	Meth/COCU
Isa. 11:1-10	Isa. 11:1-10	Isa. 11:1-10	Isa. 11:1-10	Isa. 11:1-10
Rom. 15:4-13	Rom. 15:4-9	Rom. 15:4-13	Rom. 15:4-9	Rom. 15:4-13
Matt. 3:1-12	Matt. 3:1-12	Matt. 3:1-12	Matt. 3:1-12	Matt. 3:1-12

EXEGESIS

First Lesson: Isa. 11:1-10. Isa. 11:1—12:6 consists of a series of oracles which tell of a new time of promise. The time is either toward the end of the eighth century or early in the seventh century B.C. The northern kingdom has fallen. The army of the Assyrians, God's chosen instrument of judgment, moves relentlessly toward Jerusalem. The strains of the prophetic chorus have been solemn with impending doom.

From this setting there bursts forth a new song. Isa. 11:1 picks up its opening motif from the two preceding verses. The Lord has felled all the noble forests, but now from the stump of the tree of Jesse, who was David's father and thus the *root* of the Davidic kingdom, there shall come a glorious new branch and the beginning of a wholly new era.

Vv. 2-5 describe the virtues of a new ruler. We are reminded of the birth oracles in 7:14 and 9:6-7. Similar themes are present in Ps. 72:1-4. It may well be that a liturgical pattern, perhaps used at the birth or coronation of new kings, lies behind this language.

As was true for earlier kings and prophets, the spirit (the same Hebrew word, *ruach,* also means "breath" and "wind") of the Lord provides the gifts necessary for his rule. V. 2 lists these in three pairs: what first may be described as intellectual gifts, then the practical skills necessary for rule, and finally and crucially, the means of right relationship with the Lord. (V. 3a, given in the margin of some English translations, appears to be the result of accidental repetition in the Hebrew. With the earlier six gifts, however, this formed the basis for the later Christian understanding of the seven gifts of the Holy Spirit.)

Vv. 3-5 then continue the description of the perfect king. He shall be impartial in his judgments. If anything, he will be partial to the cause of the poor and humble. True justice and integrity will be as close to him (v. 5) as his most intimate garment.

Vv. 6–9 help us to recognize that this perfection of justice and harmony takes place in a kind of mythical time. The motifs suggest the myth of return to a paradise in which no creature lived a predatory life. Just as the king was given the knowledge of the Lord (v. 2), now all the land will be filled with this knowledge.

The beginning of the next oracle (v. 10) provides a vision of a still wider hope. Picking up on v. 1, the prophet foretells how the root of Jesse will become a rallying point for the exiles of Israel and Judah. Taken by itself v. 10 even hints at the possibility of a universal kingdom of justice and peace.

Second Lesson: Rom 15:4–13. The passage comes near the conclusion of Paul's lengthy letter to the new disciples in Rome. Paul plans soon to visit them for the first time, and the letter is a form of introduction for himself and his understanding of the faith. The final chapters have offered counsel and exhortation with respect to various matters of Christian behavior, with a special stress on the unity and harmony which result from a true care and consideration for others. Paul is specifically concerned that the converts are experiencing a measure of disharmony because one group has come to regard itself as no longer needing any rules regarding such matters as foods and special days. It would appear that Paul tends to agree with this group, but he is even more interested to see that those who are *strong* in their consciences not use this strength as a way of judging and demeaning their *weaker* brothers and sisters.

Although the identification is nowhere made explicitly by Paul, some scholars believe that the gentile converts in Rome were those strong in their consciences, the Jewish Christians those weaker. In any event, a concern for all these groups plays a role in our passage. Paul has just been urging the robust in conscience to show their strength by taking into account the scruples of others. In v. 3 he quotes Ps. 69:9 to help illustrate how Christ did not put himself first but accepted reproaches which were not deservedly his. This helps to enunciate one of the most important themes of the passage: the spirit of true unity is to be realized in the imitation of Christ. The phrasing of v. 4 may suggest that there was some disagreement in Rome regarding the interpretation of the Scriptures or, perhaps, regarding which of the Scriptures were significant for Christians, or both. Briefly Paul puts forward the understanding which helped to give the Jewish Scriptures their central place in the Christian interpretation of God's purposes of salvation. *All* the Scriptures offer instruction and encouragement helping Christians to maintain hope with fortitude. The same God who is the source of these Scriptures now offers the possibility of harmony and agreement after the manner of Christ. In this awareness all may together and in unity praise God.

The manner in which Christ has accepted others is the paradigm for the Christian acceptance of one another. For the sake of the Jews Jesus became a servant (*diakonos*) in order to fulfill the promises made to the patriarchs (in the Scriptures), and he has also opened the way for the Gentiles to glorify God (vv. 7–9). To demonstrate this last point and to indicate how the Scriptures should be interpreted by Christians, Paul then quotes the OT four times: Ps. 18:49 (= 2 Sam. 22:50); Deut. 32:43; Ps. 117:1; and Isa. 11:10. The references show how this possibility has come through Judaism, so that both Jew and Gentile can praise God together.

The last quotation also helps Paul to give emphasis to the theme of hope first proclaimed to Israel in the promises of the Scriptures (v. 4). Through this hope and in the power of the Holy Spirit the joy and peace promised to Israel are being realized.

Gospel: Matt. 3:1–12. After beginning his Gospel with stories related to Jesus' birth, Matthew, like the other evangelists, presents John the Baptizer, or the Baptist, as the immediate precursor of Jesus' public ministry. An account by the contemporary Jewish writer Josephus, together with indications of John's influence upon later sectarian movements, suggests that the Baptist was a widely known figure in this time, initially perhaps far better known than Jesus. The bearers of the traditions about Jesus found it necessary both to describe Jesus' relationship to John and to make clear the greater significance of Jesus and his role. This they accomplished in several ways; but in the synoptic traditions in general, and most obviously in Matthew (3:13–15; 11:7–19; 14:1–12; 17:9–13), John becomes the Elijah-like forerunner of the Lord (originally God, but now known as Jesus). Like Mark and the Fourth Gospel, Matthew has the well-known baptizer appear suddenly on the scene. With Mark, Matthew uses an adapted form of Isa. 40:3 (in the Hebrew the voice does not cry in the wilderness but cries, "In the wilderness . . ."; and the Lord whose paths are to be made straight is specifically identified with God) to describe the purpose of John's ministry. Unlike Mark, however, Matthew omits the use of Mal. 3:1 at this point, reserving it until 11:10.

An intriguing aspect of Matthew's presentation is found in v. 2: the basic theme of Jesus' message (see 4:17; 10:7), which Mark and Luke attribute only to Jesus, is first proclaimed by John. Might Jesus have taken it over from him? "Repent [Gr. = *metanoeite,* which means "to be sorry for past sins," but more importantly, "to turn one's mind and heart to a new attitude and expectation"], for the kingdom of heaven [not a place, but God's sovereignty or ruling power] is at hand." The last phrase translates the Greek word *ēggiken,* which more literally means *"has* drawn near." Sometimes the Gospels appear to suggest that this kingdom is already fully begun in this world; at other times it seems to be just on the verge.

While vv. 1–6 are largely a Matthean adaptation of material found in Mark, vv. 7–12 come from a source used also by Luke but not by Mark. The unqualified message of repentance and impending eschatological judgment is reminiscent of OT prophecy (cf. Amos 5:18–20; Zeph. 1:14–16) and very likely conveys a proper historical sense of John's basic concerns.

While Luke presents John speaking more generally to "the multitudes," in Matthew his target is narrowed to the two best-known groups within official Judaism, the Sadducees and the Pharisees. Matthew has Jesus repeat the biting phrase "brood of vipers" in 12:34 and 23:33. This suggestion that John's denunciation was directed primarily at "the higher-ups" may reflect later Christian interpretation. Whether or not the allusion was originally intended, Christians would perceive in God's ability "from these stones to raise up children to Abraham" a reference to the opening of the kingdom to Gentiles.

Vv. 11–12 make it clear that while John announced the time of God's judgment, Jesus inaugurates this new time, in his understanding a time of hope as well. His will be more than a baptism of preparation with water. With his baptism comes the promised Spirit of the new age and the fire of the final judgment. Christian liturgical practice has, of course, integrated all these themes into one ceremony, the fire also coming to represent the presence of the Holy Spirit (so Acts 2:3). The symbolism was and continues to be rich: the water and the fire both life-threatening and life-giving forces, purifying and transforming.

HOMILETICAL INTERPRETATION

"What is faith?" asks the author of Hebrews in chap. 11. "Faith gives substance to our hopes, and makes us certain of realities we do not see" (11:1 NEB). The theme of the Scripture passages for the Second Sunday in Advent is hope, to which faith gives substance, and to both of which, faith and hope, love is essentially and inseparably joined (1 Cor. 13).

First Lesson: Isa. 11:1–10. Astonishing lines, these. They may be from Isaiah of Jerusalem, the first of the several brilliant Isaiahs who are responsible for our present Book of Isaiah; and if so, they have been in constant circulation through the human ear and eye and mind for over twenty-seven hundred years. Or this poem of bold and consummate hope may be from a later Isaiah, a disciple to the first Isaiah but distantly removed by as much as two centuries.

When one reflects on the historical probability of a continuing discipleship to Isaiah, an Isaiah *school* of prophetism, so to speak, extending at least into the latter part of the sixth century if not later, the question of precise date of such moving lines as these in Isaiah 11 becomes less important. For Isaiah and the Isaiahs, historical judgment is never an end in itself; indeed, the function of Yahweh's judgment against the people of the Covenant is cleansing, purification, renewal, making possible again the historical realization of Covenant purpose.

The purpose is of course the blessing of the families of the earth, an indomitable hope among the biblical people given support and substance in *faith*—faith in creation; faith in the promises to the ancestors (see the preceding lesson); faith in the meaning of Exodus, of Sinai, of the gift of the land; faith in the Covenant with David, one of the dominant themes in Isaiah and of course central to Isaiah 11; the Covenant word in the prophets; and for all of us who acknowledge the reality of the New Covenant, faith in the event of Jesus Christ.

Second Lesson: Rom. 15:4–13. Precisely so, as Paul says: "For *all* the ancient scriptures were written for our own instruction, in order that through the encouragement they give us we may maintain our hope with fortitude. . . . And may the God of hope fill you with all joy and peace by your faith in him, until, by the power of the Holy Spirit, you *overflow with hope*" (Rom. 15:4, 13 NEB, emphasis added).

What a work it was of the Holy Spirit to reject the Marcionite heresy in the second Christian century which then and in all subsequent centuries (it persists, but not in name, down to our own day) would cut away the OT from the life of the church! All those ancient Scriptures can conspire, especially in this season, to leave us overflowing with hope. The rehearsal, the reenactment, the celebration of the beginning of the Christ Event is an act of faith giving substance to our hope, because it came as the culmination of almost four thousand years of faith-full history in which hope was never relinquished. So Paul understood faith and hope. So did Isaiah: a shoot from the stump of Jesse, the lineage of David, would appear; and his coming would ultimately effect an absolutely incredible transformation which can be hinted at in what is symbolized in peaceful coexistence of the likes of wolf and lamb, leopard and kid, calf and lion—and all led by a little child. No more historical hurting and destroying for the sake of hurting and destroying, because the earth will be full of the knowledge of God.

In earlier lines of the Isaiah passage, the prophet tells us the one quality in this child of David which gives substance to such a hope: "He does not judge by appearances." Such judgments are surely one of our major and most disastrous problems in history to date. "He gives no verdict on hearsay [!]; but he judges the wretched *with integrity,* and *with equity* gives a verdict *for the poor*" (Isa. 11:4 JB, emphasis added).

And it is Jeremiah who lets us know what the prophet really means in speaking of the "knowledge of God." In 22:13–16, Jeremiah declares that to do justice and right, to defend the cause of the poor and needy—this is what it means to know God!

All Scripture, says Paul in effect, is ground for hope with fortitude. It is the ground of our hope now, in this season; and it is a hope inestimably enhanced by the scriptural vision of the future, both in Isaiah and the other prophets and in Paul. We have come very near letting Marxist ideology take away from us the expression of the vision of ultimate human fulfillment. We dismiss it as a "utopian dream," and let the Marxists work to achieve it. We have let this happen because of our national almost pathological anti-Communist obsession. In Advent, we need to see the prophetic vision once more. It is embraced in Paul's phrase "all scripture." The vision will fortify our hope.

Gospel: Matt. 3:1–12. It is the same kind of prophetic vision which enables John the Baptist to say and see what he does about the approaching kingdom of heaven. Talk about a ground of hope! The day will be, the day may be, the day can be when the earth will be full of the knowledge of God—the doing of justice, the elimination of all the devices and structures that inflict human hurt, human destruction, human anguish! The day will be, the day may be, the day can be when we will accept one another—in all the earth—as we know Christ accepts us! The day will be, the day may be, the day can be when we will know in our time, in our history, all that is implicit (it explodes comprehension!) in the declaration "He will baptize you with the Holy Spirit and with fire" (v. 11 RSV).

We cannot abandon the uses of utopia to Marxism and remain biblically true, true to the sense of "all scripture." Pope Paul VI once said, "Today the principal fact that we must all recognize is that the social question has become worldwide." He was speaking emphatically to the whole human family on the uses of utopia. Conceding that "the appeal to a utopia is often a convenient excuse for those who wish to escape from concrete tasks in order to take refuge in an imaginary world," he went on to say: "This kind of criticism of existing society [which utopia provides] often provokes the forward-looking imagination both to perceive in the present the disregarded possibility hidden within it, and to direct itself toward a fresh future; it thus sustains social dynamic by the confidence that it gives to the inventive powers of the human mind and heart. . . . [In the vision of utopia, the Holy Spirit] continually breaks down the horizons within which our understanding likes to find security and the limits to which our activity would willingly restrict itself; there dwells within us a power which urges us to go beyond every system and every ideology" (quoted from Joseph Gremillion, *The Gospel of Peace and Justice* [Maryknoll, N.Y.: Orbis Books, 1976], p. 502).

The Holy Spirit comes to us like fire and drives us beyond our present security to find justice and peace. Therein lies the hope proffered by Scripture. "Faith gives substance to our hopes, and makes us certain of realities we do not see." Especially in the Advent season we affirm that the earth shall be full of the knowledge of God; that we shall accept one another as Christ accepts us; and that indeed the gift to us of Christ, so soon to be freshly given again, is the gift of the Son, the Beloved of God.

The Third Sunday in Advent

Lutheran	Roman Catholic	Episcopal	Pres/UCC/Chr	Meth/COCU
Isa. 35:1-10	Isa. 35:1-6a, 10	Isa. 35:1-10	Isa. 35:1-6a, 10	Isa. 35:1-10
James 5:7-10	James 5:7-10	James 5:7-10	James 5:7-10	James 5:7-10
Matt. 11:2-11	Matt. 11:2-11	Matt. 11:2-11	Matt. 11:2-11	Matt. 11:2-11

EXEGESIS

First Lesson: Isa. 35:1-10. This poem of visionary hope stands in sharp contrast with the gloom of the preceding chapter, which pronounced God's wrath upon Edom. Because its motifs so closely parallel those of Isaiah 40—55, the vision is thought to come from that period when the Exile in Babylon was ending and from the same author or circle of prophets known to scholars as Second or Deutero-Isaiah. There, too, the return of the pilgrim people from exile is pictured as a second exodus. Once again a way is made in the desert, and God is with his people providing them with food and water in the wilderness. The transformation of the land is a vivid metaphor: it actualizes and enables the new joy and opportunity of Israel and also signifies the presence and favor of the Lord.

As in Isa. 40:29-31, the message of new hope has a special meaning for the weak and despondent (vv. 3-4). They shall know God's salvation, which will also be an act of judgment upon their enemies. Even the most unfortunate among the exiles will share in the blessings of the new day (vv. 5-6). The transformation of their handicaps will be a further sign of God's redeeming work and his justice. Moreover, their restored ability to see, to speak, to hear, and to dance will enable them to participate in the rejoicing and praise of God.

The water which springs up to create pastureland in the wilderness is again a powerful symbol suggestive of new life and God's graciousness. Not even savage animals will be present to mar this way in the converted desert.

While the general sense of v. 7 is clear, the exact translation is somewhat conjectural. The first part of the verse seems to suggest that a miragelike vision of a pool will become real. The reference to the Holy

Way or Way of Holiness (v. 8) on which the people travel to Zion (the holy temple mount in Jerusalem) perhaps contains a reminiscence of the sacred processional avenue in Babylon. But now it is the highway of those whom God has ransomed and redeemed from their exile. One again thinks of the people redeemed in the Exodus from Egypt who were called to be holy because of the holiness of their God (Lev. 20:7).

Gladness and shouts of triumph are the fitting culmination for the poem as the former exiles stream into Jerusalem. The joy or gladness they wear upon their heads may allude to the processional wreaths worn in times of great festival.

Second Lesson: James 5:7-10. The epistle is a kind of manual for Christian behavior which some scholars believe was adapted from a source or sources originally intended for a Jewish audience. Immediately preceding our passage, in 5:1-6, the author had picked up his theme of denouncing the rich, especially wealthy landlords (see 1:11-12; 2:6). This he does in no uncertain terms as he tells them of the woes which are coming upon them.

He now counsels the Christian community to patience, to which he will soon add guidance regarding steadfastness. Perhaps the writer first means that disciples must be patient because of their persecution by the rich, but as the thought moves on, he seems also to be recommending patience in the face of any sense of delay regarding the Lord's coming, and then, too, before the ordinary trials of life.

Doubtless these disciples, like many other early Christians, were experiencing some uncertainty because the years were going by and the prophesied return of Jesus had not taken place. The author does not deal with this concern as a problem, but repeats the belief (v. 8) that the coming of the Lord is near. In both vv. 7 and 8 "coming" translates the Greek word *parousia,* which became a kind of technical term for Jesus' return. The phrase "is near" translates *ēggiken* which is the verb often used in the Gospels to indicate that the kingdom of God has already drawn near.

The author uses two illustrations of patience. (A third with reference to Job is found in v. 11.) The farmer must learn to wait upon the Lord's operations in nature, in this case specifically the early (autumnal) and late (spring) rains. This pattern of rainfall is somewhat distinctive to the Palestinian area and may tell us something about the audience or the origins of this "letter," or both.

There seems to be some anxiety about the character of personal relations among these disciples, especially involving their speaking disparagingly of one another and presuming to judge others. But there is only one judge (4:12 and here in v. 9), that is, God, and his judgment is "at the door." Christians are not to judge one another. Cf. 2:12–13; 4:11–12, and recall the "judge not lest you be judged" of Matt. 7:1; Luke 6:37.

We are now given the second example of patience, this time of patience under ill-treatment or hardship. The prophets who spoke in the Lord's name were required to be patient, partly because they had to wait for the Lord to fulfill his words (which he finally did!), but also because they suffered.

The failure of the author to use Jesus as the primary example of suffering endurance (cf. 1 Pet. 2:21–24) is often remarked upon. It has been suggested that the writer regarded Jesus' suffering as unique and therefore not an apt illustration. In any event the writer is consistent in referring his readers to figures from the OT (cf. 2:21–26) as illustrations for his themes.

Gospel: Matt. 11:2–11. This passage begins a new section in Matthew's Gospel by seeking to interpret Jesus' ministry, especially in relation to that of John the Baptist. The actual historical relationship between John and Jesus was likely a complex one (see last week's Gospel) which later interpreters sought more or less to simplify, usually by identifying John as Jesus' precursor and so subordinate to him. Matthew further develops this process here. In v. 10 a version of Mal. 3:1 is employed (cf. Mark 1:2) to indicate that John is the messenger-prophet predicted in this last book of the Hebrew Scriptures.

On the basis of our evidence it is impossible to reconstruct a psychological scenario involving John's thoughts about Jesus. One can imagine, however, that there were times of doubt and uncertainty. Perhaps Jesus did not seem to proclaim God's final wrath as John thought should be done. In Matthew's presentation John is now in prison. Josephus tells us that he was imprisoned in the palace-fortress Machaerus near the eastern shore of the Dead Sea.

"The deeds of the Christ" in v. 2 is likely Matthew's expression and refers back to Jesus' activities in chaps. 8—10, to be summarized below in v. 5. "The coming one" (cf. 3:11; 21:9; 23:39) may have been a way of referring to the messiah. It could also suggest that John once thought that Jesus was the Elijah-like figure who was "to come."

Jesus' response is indirect. He claims no specific messianic designation as his own, and the reply may indicate that people must make their own faith-decision on the basis of what they see happening in association with his ministry. The signs taking place are indeed, however, the redemptive signs of the new age anticipated by the prophet Isaiah. See Isa. 29:18-19; 35:5-6; 61:1, where all these signs are prophesied, except for the raising of the dead, which may take the place of the liberation of captives in Isa. 61:1.

The stumbling block (*skandalon,* v. 6) refers to everything that makes faith difficult. Jesus here seems to indicate that he does not want any impressions about his own person or preconceived ideas about what the messiah should be like to cloud the awareness that the new age is dawning.

Jesus gives John his proper due, reminding people of what had attracted them to John in the first place. He was not some vacillating individual bending before each wind of human expectation like the rushes of the Jordan valley. Nor was he dressed like a courtier who might make people think of a royal type of messiah. Instead he behaved like what he was—a true prophet. Yet he was even more than this (and by implication Jesus is still more). John was the one predicted by Malachi, the last and greatest of prophets.

John, then, is the greatest figure of the old age. But the new age has now dawned, and "the least in the kingdom" is greater than he. This latter phrase may be Jesus' modest way of referring to himself; or it may refer to any disciple, who now, according to the inferences throughout this passage, must choose between following Jesus or John.

HOMILETICAL INTERPRETATION

The first text, Isaiah 35, is a lyrical declaration of the divine intention in the act of redemption: the blind will see, the deaf will hear, the lame will leap, and the dumb will sing! Limitations and distortions and inhibitions of vision and understanding and comprehension and insight, and of movement, and of articulation and communication—these accompaniments of a "captive" existence will be taken away. And *of course* the earth will be transformed, since the redeemed will see it, apprehend it, experience it, with faculties for the first time unfettered.

The second text in James 5:7-10, no less certain that the event of redemption will be, that it is in fact en route, and that one may (and must) live in the assurance of its reality, nevertheless admonishes patience—such as the farmer must possess when planting in confidence of the coming of nourishing rain, or such as the prophets exhibit when they endure public derision for their insistence that the Word of God will be fulfilled.

And Matt. 11:2-11 underscores the vast qualitative difference between life outside and inside the "kingdom," between what precedes and what follows the event of redemption, between what characterizes human life before and after entrance into the realm of God.

First Lesson: Isa. 35:1-10. To read this passage aloud is a high achievement of faith, sensitivity, and beauty. If you have persons in your congregation of genuine dramatic gift, have one of them—or two of them in an antiphonal recital—read the chapter. For a number of decades now in biblical studies there has been increasing awareness of the prominent, persistent role of oral composition and communication of ancient texts, especially in the case of prophetic poetry. When we reproduce a passage like Isaiah 35 by voice and transmit it from mouth to ear, we return the text to its earliest form of creation and transmission.

Do you have easily at hand and preferably on your desk several translations of the Bible? There is no law which proscribes our employing more than one translation in the reading of a given text (and if you can use Hebrew and Greek in making a decision between variant translations, so much the better). A perusal of Isaiah 35 in several "Bibles" will be highly productive. (Read it aloud in your own study!) Use the RSV, of course, and the King James; but put the older, more conventional, probably more familiar text over against the New English Bible (NEB) or the Jerusalem Bible (JB); or another relatively recent Roman Catholic translation, the New American Bible (NAB); or the still more recent Good News Bible: The Bible in Today's English Version (TEV).

Suppose, for example, we look at different ways in which the final line of the poem is rendered—and it is right that one be free to make one's own choice.

RSV: They [the redeemed] shall obtain joy and gladness, / and sorrow and sighing shall flee away.

JB: Joy and gladness will go with them / and sorrow and lament be ended.

NEB: Gladness and joy shall be their escort, / and suffering and weariness shall flee away.

NAB: They will meet with joy and gladness, / sorrow and mourning will flee.

TEV: They will be happy forever, / forever free from sorrow and grief.

Subtle—and perhaps substantive—differences in reading are here, providing an authoritative range in theological, literary, and aesthetic choice!

Maybe your own creation of a fresh rendering of Isaiah 35 ought to be in fact a part of the sermon for this Third Sunday in Advent!

Second Lesson: James 5:7–10. Consider the epistle's invocation of the prophetic model as inspiration and support for patience and, by inference, for the maintenance of faith in the Word of redemption. What lies behind it? Prior to the fall first of the northern kingdom in 722/21 B.C. and then the southern kingdom in 587/86, the prophets were held up for ridicule for proclaiming Yahweh's word of judgment. But since in the great prophets of the classical period from the eighth through the sixth centuries it was predominately a word of judgment for the sake of making possible redemption, public derision and even persecution of the prophets were *in reality* directed against the prophetic proclamation of the Word as such, against the fundamental prophetic conviction of the actual presence of the Holy-One-in-our-midst, of God-in-our-time, of God-by-Word, effecting God's will for the ultimate blessing of all the families of the earth.

This rejection of God as ultimate Redeemer lies back of the anguish of Jeremiah, for example, when he describes the Word of Yahweh as an unwanted fire shut up in his bones (see Jer. 20:7–9); or Isaiah's frustration when he lives in the midst of a people whose refrain has become, "Let us hear no more of the Holy One of Israel" (see Isa. 30:8–11).

We Christian folk, a minority in the world, insist especially in this season that the God-Word of redemption has not only been spoken in the prophets but *given* in Jesus Christ; and we must exercise the prophetic patience spoken of in the epistle as an increasingly derisive world taunts us in bitter sarcasm, "How long, O Lord, how long?" We are called to believe the redemptive Word, in faith to reenact the coming of that Word in the flesh, and with prophetic persistence not only to insist that it is *now coming* but that it is possible for us to live now as if redemption were the kind of actuality so lyrically described in Isaiah 35.

Gospel: Matt. 11:2–11. According to our Gospel text in Matthew 11, John the Baptist, in prison, sends disciples, his own, to ask of Jesus who he really is. "Are you he who is to come, or shall we look for another?" (v. 3 RSV). Jesus responds, not in terms of himself, of his own person, of his commission or authority, but by a simple, unadorned enumeration of some of the central elements in the prophetic vision of the coming Day and the coming One, characteristic of his own ministry: (1) the blind see, (2) the lame walk, (3) lepers are cured, (4) the deaf hear, (5) the dead are raised, and (6) the poor have good news preached to them.

Several of these phenomena appear in Isaiah 35 in the prophet's vision of the redemption that is about to be: the blind will see (1); the deaf will hear (4); the lame will leap (2); and it is possible that the singing of the dumb in Isaiah is related to Matthew's healing of lepers (3) and raising of the dead (5). Matthew's note of good news to the poor (6) is, as we have already suggested, strongly implicit in Isaiah 35.

Note the two other Isaiah texts cited in the exegesis where these same qualities of the redeemed age are identified: Isa. 29:18-19; Isa. 61:1-3. (See exegesis.) In Luke 4:16-21, Jesus reads from Isaiah 61 and then declares, "Today . . . in your very hearing, this text has come true" (v. 21 NEB). The word back to John the Baptist is unmistakably clear: You will look for no other because prophetic hope and expectation in "that Day" is even now being fulfilled. These texts have come true.

We still live in hope and expectation of the Day. But in this season, in faith and prophetic patience, we celebrate and recreate the inauguration of the day, the entrance into time and the now ineradicable presence among us of that which brings healing to all manner of human obtuseness, limitation, scourge, and folly. And indeed we know, as all three of our texts testify, that in the midst of death, we are in life.

The Fourth Sunday in Advent

Lutheran	Roman Catholic	Episcopal	Pres/UCC/Chr	Meth/COCU
Isa. 7:10-14 (15-17)	Isa. 7:10-14	Isa. 7:10-17	Isa. 7:10-15	Isa. 7:10-17
Rom. 1:1-7	Rom. 1:1-7	Rom. 1:1-7	Rom. 1:1-7	Rom. 1:1-7
Matt. 1:18-25	Matt. 1:18-24	Matt. 1:18-25	Matt. 1:18-25	Matt. 1:18-25

EXEGESIS

First Lesson: Isa. 7:10-17. It is 735 B.C. Assyria has become the dominant power in the Middle East and is threatening Judah and her near neighbors Syria (or Aram) and the northern kingdom Israel (or

Ephraim). Syria and Israel in turn are menacing King Ahaz of Judah unless he joins them in an alliance against Assyria. The prophet has just issued an oracle (7:1–9) assuring Ahaz that he need not fear Syria and Israel since they will soon be destroyed.

In the Lord's name Isaiah now speaks again to Ahaz in the presence of the royal court ("house of David," v. 13). His purpose is to cause Ahaz to trust in God alone and not in political intrigue. He offers the king a sign (*'oth*) of God's care and readiness to defend Judah. Ahaz, who has likely already decided to seek a pact with Assyria, refuses the offer with pious rhetoric (v. 12); he would not put the Lord to the test. He thus shows his lack of faith and has now worn out the patience of both the prophet and his God. A sign will be given whether Ahaz wants one or not.

The precise meaning of the next verses is much debated. The sign is that a young woman will bear a son who will be called Immanuel, which means "God is with us." The Hebrew word *'almah* means a woman who has reached marriageable age. There seems to be no intention to specify that she was a virgin (as the Greek word *parthenos* used in translation would indicate), although neither is that possibility ruled out.

The identity of the woman and the boy is uncertain. Most often she is thought to be one of Ahaz's wives whose offspring (perhaps the next king, Hezekiah) will demonstrate God's faithfulness in fulfilling his promise to preserve the Davidic dynasty (2 Sam. 7:12–16; Ps. 89). The sign could then also relate to the birth oracle in 9:6–7.

The sign may, however, refer to the prophetess, the wife of Isaiah, who will soon bear a son whose name signifies "speedy-spoil-quick booty" (8:1–4). Other interpreters see here a reference to the ideal king who will some day come, thus encouraging the later Christian messianic interpretation. It may also be that the prophet had in mind any woman who would have the faith in the future to give birth at this time.

In any event, this is a strangely mixed period of both hope and judgment. Judah will temporarily be saved, although then finally devastated (v. 17). By the time the child is old enough to show the first signs of teachability, Syria-Israel's threat will be done with. The significance of the phrase referring to curds and honey is variously interpreted. It could again refer to the child's development, suggesting that the child will grow quickly because of his diet. It may mean that he and/or the people of Judah will soon have this diet, which could signify either abundance (these were the delicacies of a nomadic people) or scarcity (for only the food of nomads will be available).

Second Lesson: Rom. 1:1-7. The opening verses are an expansion of the normal introduction of a Greek letter, which gives the names of the sender and recipient and a brief word of greeting. This introduction is also more elaborate than those found in any other of Paul's letters, probably due to the fact that he is writing to a community whom he has not yet met but plans soon to visit. The first seven verses are densely packed with pregnant words and phrases requiring delicate translation and interpretation.

Paul is a "servant" of Christ Jesus. The word *doulos* might more literally be translated 'slave,' but Paul does not mean the slavery of ownership so much as the servanthood of obedience (cf. v. 5). The word is a complement to the designation of Jesus as Lord. On Paul's calling to be an *apostle* ("one who is sent," and also a witness to Jesus and his resurrection) see especially Gal. 1:1—2:10; 1 Cor. 9:1. Paul did not receive this appointment through human agency but directly from Jesus. So was he *set apart* for the *euangelion* of God. This gospel Paul understands here to be specifically the good news about Jesus together with Paul's special commission to bring it to all nations (v. 5). Nor is this gospel some accident of history. Paul attests his belief that its promise can be perceived to have been prophesied in the Jewish Scriptures (v. 2).

Vv. 3-4 may have their basis in an early Christian creed. This statement sets forth a way of thinking of Jesus as both human and "of God." A crucial word is *horisthentos* in v. 4, meaning "designated," "installed," or perhaps "declared" Son of God. While from one perspective (*kata sarka,* "according to the flesh") Jesus was fully human and from the messianic line of David, by power according to (*kata*) the "Spirit of holiness" (presumably meaning the Holy Spirit) Jesus was "designated" Son of God. This sonship was designated or declared by (*ex,* meaning either "because of" or "at the time of") resurrection from the dead. In the space of this one verse (v. 4) Paul refers to Jesus as Christ, as Son of God (although not yet used in a metaphysical sense, here meaning he was uniquely related to God), and as Lord. Jesus is worthy of all these titles, and all of them together cannot fully tell who he is. They belong to his name, not he to them (v. 5). The gospel is Jesus.

Paul's special commission is to bring people of all nations to a faith leading to obedience. This *faith* is, of course, a crucial theme of the letter.

Finally, after so describing himself and Jesus as his Lord, Paul tells the Roman disciples who they are: they are beloved of God and "called to be saints"—that is, "holy people"—because of their calling. To them be *grace* (which may represent a Christianization of a common Greek greeting) and *peace* (the common Semitic salutation) from God the Father, with whom in the giving of this grace and peace the Lord Jesus Christ is now intimately associated.

Gospel: Matt. 1:18-25. After beginning his Gospel with a genealogy showing that Jesus comes from the lineage of King David and ultimately of Abraham, Matthew tells of the birth of the Christ (or Messiah)—how it is both of God through Mary and yet through descent from Joseph by God's action as well.

Matthew's narrative has several important features in common with Luke's infancy story, most especially the conception by a virgin woman, Mary, through the activity of the Holy Spirit. Such features indicate traditions about Jesus' birth which existed prior to the work of both evangelists. They were either unknown to Mark, John, Paul, and other NT writers or not regarded as of the same significance.

There are also many differences between the stories of Matthew and Luke. Most noticeable in our passage is the fact that the narrative is told from Joseph's point of view rather than Mary's. Matthew's story is at least as much concerned with telling us how Joseph's qualms were overcome, enabling him to take Mary into his home (so making Jesus the legitimate son of David), as it is with the birth of Jesus *per se.* For people of that time this way of understanding parentage would have been far more important than any concerns with physical descent.

The evangelist does not tell us how Mary learned of the conception by the Holy Spirit—more literally, "by a holy Spirit"; that is, by God's divine power. (Matthew does not personify the Spirit.) Jesus' birth was thus understood to have come about through both human and divine agency. We are reminded of the birth narratives involving Sarah, Rebekah, and Hannah in the OT.

Joseph is both a *righteous* man (concerned to live according to the law) and compassionate. He decides he must break the betrothal contract yet wishes to do it as discreetly as possible. But he is visited by an angel in a dream. Both the angel and the dream were means of divine revelation and guidance. Joseph is to take Mary home as his wife and to name the child Jesus, which Matthew understands to signify that "he will save his people from their sins." The name in Hebrew *Yeshua* (a shortening of *Yehoshua* = Joshua), meaning "Yahweh helps," was popularly understood to mean "Yahweh saves."

V. 22 makes use of a formula frequently employed by Matthew to introduce an OT quotation which he perceives to be fulfilled in Jesus' story. On the background of Isa. 7:14, see the First Lesson. Although the Greek word *parthenos* does not require the meaning "virgin" in a technical sense, this is its normal usage, and it is so understood by Matthew. Jesus' birth thus comes to be regarded as miraculous in a manner which bears similarities to the geneses of several heroes of the pagan world.

HOMILETICAL INTERPRETATION

The quality of faith is a common feature of all three texts. In Isaiah 7, the king (Ahaz) is admonished to trust the Word of God through the word of the prophet. Ahaz declines to do so. In Romans 1, it is faith that persuades Paul of the authenticity of his commission: faith in the prophetic Word of the coming, long in advance, of this Son of David; faith that he, Paul, was "set apart" by Another; faith that his mission was to all nations; and faith that the creation of faith was the substance of his mission. In Matt. 1:18–25 it is Joseph's faith in the Word of an angel which he heard in a dream that—humanly speaking—made possible the subsequent narratives of Jesus, son of Joseph and Mary.

It may be well to take time to put all three texts in total biblical context. The authentic, human, catholic (universal) appeal of the Bible lies in its central, thematic, pervasive, indomitable quality of faith, of trust, of belief. Abraham *believed* God, who accounted the quality of belief to him in lieu of a righteousness which neither Abraham nor anyone else is able to achieve (see Gen. 15:6). The people of Sarah and Abraham, Rebekah and Isaac, Leah and Rachel and Jacob survived the hard centuries because they believed (to be sure in the midst of chronic disbelief, unbelief) the Word of God that somehow, ultimately, they would be instrumental in the blessing of the families of the earth. The theme of faith, more often implicit than explicit, literally carries the history of the OT, and without it the fabulous story of the gospel would hardly have achieved the status even of dream.

First Lesson: Isa. 7:10–17. To say that the prophet Isaiah of Jerusalem (the first, eighth-century Isaiah) is unique among the prophets is not in itself to single him out, since the same must be said of each of that unique company of prophets from Amos to the later Isaiahs. While they are all clearly indebted to common traditions and, in notable instances, to each other, they nevertheless stand out boldly each as his own person, each distinctive in his own way.

Yet words have been spoken of Isaiah which put him in a class by himself even in such a distinctive company of radical individuals as the classical prophets. If any prophet is to be ranked under the amorphous and otherwise undefined category of "greatest" of the prophets, it would certainly be Isaiah. And if the category of "theologian" is applicable to the prophets, then beyond dispute Isaiah is the greatest prophetic theologian.

Preaching involves inevitably a teaching function; and there is a relationship between the vitality of the church and the biblical literacy of its membership. Isaiah, for example, is someone every church member should know; and to know him is to know something about him in relation to his time, his contemporaries, his colleagues.

The late Gerhard von Rad of Heidelberg, one of my teachers, a cherished older friend and colleague and a person as theologically sensitive in his own way as Isaiah himself, goes so far in praise of Isaiah as to say that "the preaching of Isaiah represents the theological high watermark of the whole Old Testament. . . . Not one of the other prophets approaches Isaiah in intellectual vigor or, more particularly, in the magnificent sweep of his ideas" (my translation from the original German text of his *Theologie des alten Testaments* [Munich: Christian Kaiser Verlag, 1960] 2:158).

And in nothing is the distinctive Isaiah more distinctive than in his understanding and use of the concept of faith. Look at it! Our text for the day, 7:10–17, is permeated with the notion of faith. It isn't any wonder that the early church, reading "virgin" for "young woman," identified Jesus Christ as the expected child whose name would be Immanuel, meaning "God is with us." (See the discussion of the historicity of the episode in the exegesis above.) In addition to possible contemporary historical identities for Immanuel, some suggest a *third* child of Isaiah, in addition to Shear-jashub, 7:3, and Maher-shalal-hash-baz, 8:3 (Did he live a lifetime with that name?). And whatever the immediate historical expectation in the time of Isaiah and Ahaz, we have to say in faith that in any ultimate sense only Christ fulfills the name and expectation.

Let's go to the Isaian context of our text. A quick rereading of Isaiah 1 will tell you that for Isaiah, as Isaiah sees his time (and all time?), Jerusalem and Judah (and all of humankind?) know a total and pervasive sickness. The sickness in and of itself is fatal since it results from the willful, prideful breach of the one relationship in which alone life and health inhere—our relationship with God. It must be said that in the faith of the Isaiahs, restoration lies only beyond catastrophe, and it may come only from the recovery of that lost relationship, in the child's trust of the parent's trustworthiness, the confidence of the patient in the competence of the physician, the faith of the hearer of Yahweh's Word in the faithfulness of Yahweh.

Notice the implications of *faith* in Isaiah:

7:9. "If you will not believe, surely you shall not be established" (RSV). (Or NEB, picking up on the Hebrew play on words): 'Have firm faith, or you will not stand firm.'

28:16. One who believes (that is, the believer) "will not be in haste"; or (NEB) "shall not waver." Perhaps even better (the text in Hebrew presents a difficult word), "One who believes will not be anxious." If you know German, here is a superb reading: *Wer da glaubt, nicht wird er aufgeregt sein* ("Whoso believes will not be [inwardly] moved"). Paul in Rom. 10:11 Christianizes (legitimately) the text when he quotes: "Everyone who has faith in him [Christ] will be saved from shame" (NEB).

Elsewhere in the Book of Isaiah the same root, *'mn,* or *amn* (from whence our *amen*), is repeatedly used to testify to the worthiness, the dependability, the faithfulness of the object of faith.

11:5. Here the shoot from the stump of Jesse (the Davidic ruler to come) wears as intimate clothing righteousness and—here is our word— "faithfulness, total trustworthiness" (*amn*).

In 25:1, Yahweh's plans formed of old are absolutely faithful, unqualifiedly dependable. The same root, *amn,* is used twice to give superlative force.

33:6. Yahweh will be the stability (from *amn*) of your times.

49:7. Yahweh is faithful (from *amn*), that is, worthy of trust.

55:3. Here are two words difficult to render, but the sense is sure: The mercies of David—that is, Yahweh's promises in and through David—are to be believed (again, from *amn*); they are sure, they are worthy of trust; they have substance, stability.

And in 26:2 the gates are to be opened—to whom? To the righteous. But who are these righteous? They are the keepers of faithfulness (from *amn*), they who keep faith, they who live in faith.

Those who live in faith enter the open gates beyond the fires of the furnace and the waters of the flood, with the sickness of their life healed, their pride relinquished, their rebelliousness blotted out and forgiven, and the fundamental relationship of their life restored, renewed, redeemed.

Precisely in Immanuel, "God with us"—in Christ.

Second Lesson: Rom. 1:1-7. Who is Paul? In matters that really matter, who is Paul—who are you, who am I, who, indeed, are the people we serve in ministry? We may not "make" it, but Paul answers for himself and for all of us who own the name Christian when he says, so simply, so powerfully, so devastatingly, "[1] Servant of Christ Jesus, [2] apostle by God's call, [3] set apart for the service of the Gospel" (NEB). There are some bold claims for you!

What is the validation of all this? The validation is itself an act of faith, faith in the Word of God in Scripture, faith in the Word of God to, in, and through the prophets. *Amn.* We are talking about God's Son (v. 3), Immanuel; we are talking about One born of David's stock, from the root of Jesse, David's father (Isa. 11); and we are talking about One who comes of the Holy Spirit—ask a sign of Yahweh your God as deep as Sheol or as high as heaven!

This is the substance of Paul's commission—and ours. Can we believe it? Do we trust (*amn*) it?

Gospel: Matt. 1:18-25. The response of faith shifts from Isaiah and his disciples to Paul, and now to Joseph. NEB takes a little liberty with the Greek text but the statement is true to Matthew's sense of things: "This is the story of the birth of the Messiah" (a not illegitimate rendering of "Jesus Christ"). It is of course a statement absolutely inconceivable apart from the prophetic Word—and apart from the quality of faith.

And the closing of our text would in the same light be equally inconceivable: "Joseph did as the angel had directed him . . ." (v. 24 NEB).

And this, colleague in ministry, colleague in the church, is the hard question of our texts: Can we keep company in faith with the likes of Isaiah and Paul and Joseph? And if so, how do we do it? How else than by validating—by accepting as authentic and authoritative—the Word of God, *Immanuel*, to prophet, to Joseph, to Paul, to evangelist, and to us.

The Nativity of Our Lord, Christmas Day

Lutheran	Roman Catholic	Episcopal	Pres/UCC/Chr	Meth/COCU
Isa. 9:2-7	Isa. 9:2-7	Isa. 9:2-4, 6-7	Isa. 9:2, 6-7	Isa. 9:1-7
Titus 2:11-14	Titus 2:11-14	Titus 2:11-14	Titus 2:11-15	Titus 2:11-15
Luke 2:1-20	Luke 2:1-14	Luke 2:1-14 (15-20)	Luke 2:1-14	Luke 2:1-20

EXEGESIS

First Lesson: Isa. 9:2-7. (Note: In some translations, which follow the enumeration of the Hebrew Bible, these verses are numbered 9:1-6.) The passage is found in the midst of a series of oracles of judgment. The lands of Zebulun and Naphtali in the northern kingdom of Israel have been overrun by the Assyrians (cf. v. 1). Everywhere there is distress and darkness (8:22). To these circumstances the prophet speaks offering a great light of new hope. God will raise up a new king for the throne of David who will lead the nation to victory and restore the borders of the ancient kingdom.

The oracle is probably modeled on liturgical language used at the coronation of new kings, which was spoken of as like the "birth" of a new son (of God). See Ps. 2:7. It is possible, however, that the prophet was thinking more literally of the actual birth of a new heir. In any event, this vision of new hope should be read in association with 7:14 and 11:1-10, the other great birth oracles of Isaiah.

If the prophet had a historical individual in mind, Hezekiah, who came to the throne in 715, is the only suitable figure. While many scholars continue to believe that the prophecy was formulated with an ideal king as its focus, the two possibilities are not necessarily mutually exclusive. Each time a new king came to the throne, there was likely an upsurge of hope and a sense of new opportunity. Hard realism recognized, however, that the new monarch would have his failings and suffer from the historical constraints of his circumstances. Thus the vision would look beyond him to the perfect ruler who would come at the end of history. Christians, of course, viewed the time of Jesus in this light. See Matt. 4:15-16; Luke 1:79.

The opening line of v. 3 probably should be read following the NEB or NAB rather than the RSV. The joy of the new day is first described in terms of agricultural imagery and then with reference to a great military victory, after which all the gear and bloody reminders of war are burned. It will be as when Midian was defeated by Israel. See Judg. 7:15-25.

Following the custom of the time, the new king is given four crown *names* which describe his virtues. He will have wisdom, courage in battle, and fatherly care, and he will bring about prosperity and harmony. He is literally "wonder of a counselor" (recalling King Solomon). He is "mighty divine being," a hero-warrior; that is, because he is God's Son he can be given the divine attribute. He is like a father to his people, a father forever, with an eternal character. Finally, he is prince of peace (= *shalom* = "fullness, completion, harmony"), which peace (see in v. 7) is not just the absence of war but the presence of justice and righteousness.

The last line of the oracle is a reminder that it is not by political intrigue or other human effort that this will happen. The jealous zeal of Yahweh Sabaoth will establish this new kingdom.

Second Lesson: Titus 2:11-15. As a young man Titus was a companion and trusted friend of Paul. This letter pictures Paul writing to Titus, who now has a role of leadership in the Christian community on the Island of Crete. Most scholars believe that the letter was actually written in Paul's name at some point after his death in order to convey what it was felt that Paul would say were he still alive. The author is mostly interested in matters of pastoral concern and discipline. Both his reason for concern and the source of strength for right living are given in our passage. Christians live between the two appearances (*epiphanies,* vv. 11, 13) of Christ—first in his incarnation, and then in his coming again.

"Grace" in v. 11 refers rather generally to God's gracious act in Jesus and not to Paul's more dynamic concept. This has been given for the healing-salvation (the Greek word is cognate with Savior) of all people. There is perhaps some hint of the "to Gentiles as well as Jews" theme.

There may be an allusion to baptism in the pattern of first renouncing "godless" ways and then affirming "godly" ones. Christians can do this "in this age" because of their "blessings-bringing" (Gr. *makarian*) hope in the new age or world to come, which shall be inaugurated with an epiphany of glory (= *doxa*) of the great God and our Savior Jesus Christ. The best translation for this last phrase is debated (note the margins of most versions), since it appears to call Jesus God without qualification, an attribution which is at least somewhat anomalous throughout the NT period. Grammatical considerations and the fact that it is *Jesus'* appearance and saving work which are the focus of discussion suggest, however, that the author did mean to refer to Jesus as God. The title *Savior* can be used independently for both Christ and God in these epistles (see Titus 3:4 with 3:6). Here, perhaps influenced by the use of the phrase "God and Savior" to describe the divinity of emperor figures in the Hellenistic world, especially when they made their *epiphanies* or grand appearances on state occasions, Jesus is presented as himself divine, even though the author probably did not intend to put forward some direct equation with the divinity of the Father-God.

Christians can lead the disciplined life because of what Christ did at his first appearing. He gave himself for us to redeem (= *lutrōmai* = "ransom") us from iniquity (literally "lawlessness," the opposite of a disciplined life). So did he cleanse or purify for himself a people of his own. The last phrase seems an allusion to the holy people of God, now viewed as the new Israel (1 Pet. 2:9–10).

Gospel: Luke 2:1–14. After telling of the conception of John and Jesus, of Mary's visit to Elizabeth, and then of John's birth, Luke now presents the story of Jesus' nativity. This material is unique to his Gospel and is composed in the evangelist's own prose style. The narrative, simple on its surface, is an artful weaving together of perspectives. The birth takes place among the rude circumstances of human history but is cosmic in its significance; it is at once natural and supernatural. The child, whose place of birth was dictated both by the plan of God foretold by the prophets and the seeming accident of the actions of the government of the Hellenistic world, will one day be recognized as the Savior and Lord (both predominantly Hellenistic titles) of that world, as well as being known to be the promised Messiah of Judaism. (See v. 11 where all three of these designations are used.)

Although interesting attempts have been made to solve the problem created by Luke in these first verses concerning the date of Jesus' birth, it would seem that the evangelist was more interested in the theological and symbolic significance of his narrative than in what we would regard as historical accuracy. Both Matthew and Luke 1:5 date these events during the lifetime of King Herod, who died in 4 B.C. Quirinius, however, did not become the Roman legate, or governor, of Syria until 6 A.D. Josephus also knows of some form of an enrollment for tax purposes in Palestine about this time (and cf. Acts 5:37), but we are told nothing by historians of the period of any earlier census—certainly not one involving the whole empire. Luke's major purpose, however, is to deal with the traditions which associate Jesus' infancy both with the obscure Galilean town of Nazareth and with Bethlehem, the city of David, in which it was prophesied that the new ruler of Israel would be born (Mic. 5:2).

The contract of betrothal (v. 5) was in many ways more important than marriage itself. Luke understands Mary to have conceived as a virgin (1:34), but Joseph, from whom the Davidic lineage comes, is Jesus' father in every other way. The child is the "first-born" (*prototokos*, cf. 2:23), a term rich in background, signifying in Judaism the heir and favorite child. But this baby is born in circumstances of simplicity, with an animal trough for a crib, because there was no place for them in "the guest room" (of an inn? or perhaps near a cave where they may have been staying?). One thinks of Luke 9:58—the Son of man with no place to lay his head—and of 2 Cor. 8:9—"for your sake he became poor." It may be, however, that the traditional interpretation stressing the poverty of Jesus' birth is largely based on a later romantic reading of the narrative. Some scholars contend that Luke is only describing the peculiarity of the nativity's location as it was dictated by circumstances and that several of the details are meant to show how well the baby was cared for despite the difficulties.

An angel brings to shepherds the "good news" (v. 10) concerning the Savior and the sign of his being "wrapped in swaddling cloths and lying in a manger" (v. 12 RSV). There is at least some irony here; many would expect something much more magnificent. Then, too, shepherds were regarded by many as outcasts because their work did not allow them to fulfill all the obligations of their religion. The angel's words recall similar announcements to Zechariah (1:13–17) and Mary (1:28–33), especially in the manner in which their initial awe or terror must be overcome with joy (an important Lucan motif). The glory which shines about the shepherds is reminiscent of the Lord's glory at the great salvation event of the Exodus (Exod. 14:4, 18; 16:7).

While there is a textual problem and some question of translation in the last verse, most modern versions have the sense correctly. The "peace" (passing human understanding) comes upon those whom God favors. This is his doing and not the result of any mortal effort. The hosts of heaven sing God's praise, and the passage closes on this quasi-liturgical note.

HOMILETICAL INTERPRETATION

What are some of the themes that sing out in our three texts? (No Christmas sermon can treat them all!) If in faith, if in light of the

Christ Event we read Isa. 9:2-7 as giving color and content and meaning to God's invasion of human history in Jesus Christ, then long before the Coming, prophetic consciousness sang out lyrically of human redemption in the Person of a child—redemption *from* darkness and death; *from* oppression; *from* the ravages of war; redemption *to* peace and justice and righteousness.

In the Letter to Titus 2:11-15, we are as it were between Comings. The first, completed Christ Event is described as the *grace* of God which has dawned upon the world with healing for all humankind (cf. NEB); and in the light of this Event, we are called (or instructed, or disciplined) to live temperately, justly, and devoutly until the second Coming in *glory*. Isaiah 9 is echoed; and one thinks of the line in Mic. 6:8 which calls us to do justly, to love mercy, and to walk humbly with God.

Luke 2:1-14 is another birth narrative (with Matt. 2). It purports to take us to the very scene of the Coming; but like Isaiah and Titus, this text too sings of the meaning of the event—peace, as God wills to give peace.

First Lesson: Isa. 9:2-7. What does it mean, what does it really mean, this Coming of the Christ-child two thousand years ago? To some, probably even to most who share our time, it means nothing at all. The substance of Christmas is for many as insubstantial as the stuff of prophets' vision and shepherds' dreams.

The meaning is sharply defined in Isaiah (or one of his disciples). It means the fulfillment of God's promise to bless through the people and history of ancient Israel all the families of the earth. The instrument of blessing is not now the nation, Israel, but *one* from the nation (but in the Hebraic concept of the one in the many and the many in the one, all Israel is embraced); one in the Davidic succession; one on "David's throne" who will come, of course, as a child, a boy, a Son; one who will come as Liberator and Redeemer of all who walk in a darkness that is deathlike. Misery, despondency, frustration, unfulfillment, all manner of dehumanization (by inference) will give way to joy and gladness. The yoke of human oppression, forced in how many different forms on the shoulders of the living, will be broken. This always *is* the meaning of the Event. The vast paraphernalia of mutual human destruction will be no more, and the resulting quality of human life is symbolized in the titles of the Son who is given us. Peace, boundless peace (NEB), will result from the permanent achievement of justice and righteousness. This is the meaning of the Event in Isaiah 9.

Second Lesson: Titus 2:11-15. What does it mean, what does it really mean, this coming of the Christ-child two thousand years ago? There are those—we know them—who take the Event as a divine guarantee that all is and will be well *with them.* In Jesus Christ, God gives *them* peace.

What does Christmas mean? Not this. Christ was proclaimed by folk, all kinds of folk, who believed him to be the love of God come into a bitter, broken world. His coming, in and of itself, was never seen as miraculously effecting the cure of the world's ills. The world's brokenness and humankind's multiple, bitter divisions were to be faced with new hope and courage in the fresh knowledge of God's love, and of the phenomenal measure of that love introduced in Jesus Christ.

So the Letter to Titus. "The grace of God has dawned upon the world [in the gift of a Son] with healing for *all* . . ." (2:11 NEB, emphasis added). If we are healed in the Coming, we are all the more obligated to the tasks of healing. The Coming calls us, instructs us (TEV), disciplines us (NEB), trains us (RSV and NAB), to live temperately, justly, and devoutly in a new simplicity of life, with renewed passion for justice in a world where injustice is rampant, and in commitment to the will of God supremely revealed in the Person and the Event.

Christmas, freighted with so much, but so clear in essential meaning. I once tried to say it in sonnet form:

> The Season brings back all the seasons past.
> The Christmases of every other year
> Invest this time and charge it with a vast
> And melancholy sense of poignant cheer.
>
> Where, and with whom? How many years before?
> And now again we sing the songs, release
> Our trembling fears: "O Come, let us adore"
> The Christmas child who comes to bring us peace.
>
> The loves of other years invest the time;
> The wars of other years, and human hells,
> The bloody, brutal contradictions chime
> This year as loud as peace among the bells.
>
> So, Peace on Earth! But in this world of sin,
> He comes to call on us to bring Peace in.

Gospel: Luke 2:1-14. Joseph went from Nazareth to the city of David, Bethlehem. Mary, pregnant, went with him; and while they were there, Mary "gave birth to a son, her first-born. She wrapped him in his swaddling clothes, and laid him in a manger, because there was no room for them to lodge in the house" (Luke 2:7 NEB).

Looked at against the simplicity of Luke's account, the commercialization of Christmas is scandalous. But this ought not to blow our theological mind as much as the perennial bumper sticker which proclaims, "Keep Christ in Christmas." Why should we, if we have lost love in our lives? If Christmas has become a scandal, it isn't a particular scandal. It's a part of the total scandal of our driven, frenetic existence. It belongs to the scandal of our general loss of human values.

Maybe there's a sense in which the very display of our cheaper values is appropriate. The Event of Christmas reaffirms the invasion and conquest of the ornate by the simple, of power by the powerless, of grossness by sensitivity, of exploitation by guilelessness, of alienation by love. If in this season our human gifts of art and music and poetry, affection and mythology and gospel appear as commercially cheapened in contrast to the Event, it is on the other hand astonishing that the inherent beauty of the celebration cannot be smothered.

What does it mean, what does it really mean, this coming of the Christ-child two thousand years ago? If we sing of peace, of goodwill, of the love of God in Christ, we do not suppose that this is some magic incantation, itself producing and insuring a good and a whole world. We receive Christ in the midst of a corporate human life largely empty of him, and of the love of God, and of peace and goodwill.

What does it mean? Not what the red, green, silver, and gold celebration would suggest. And of course the amazing thing about it is that the whole gaudy show at its very worst never succeeds in suppressing the real meaning of the Event. The Person breaks through; and as in every age, wise men and shepherds, the sophisticated and the simple, are able to reaffirm in their own language that only in the Child, the Son, the given, simple, gentle, powerless Person, lies our peace and our salvation.

The First Sunday after Christmas

Lutheran	Roman Catholic	Episcopal	Pres/UCC/Chr	Meth/COCU
Isa. 63:7-9	Sir. 3:2-6, 12-14	Isa. 61:10—62:3	Eccles. 3:1-9, 14-17	Isa. 63:7-9 or Eccles. 3:1-9, 14-17 or Sir. 3:2-6, 12-14
Gal. 4:4-7	Col. 3:12-21	Gal. 3:23-25; 4:4-7	Col. 3:12-17	Gal. 4:4-7
Matt. 2:13-15, 19-23	Matt. 2:13-15, 19-23	John 1:1-18	Matt. 2:13-15, 19-23	John 1:1-18

EXEGESIS

First Lesson: Isa. 63:7-9. The first six verses of chap. 63 are a dialogue between the prophet, acting as a watchman for Israel, and the Lord, portrayed as a mighty warrior who has just triumphed over his people's enemies. Vv. 7-9 then begin a section of praise proclaimed by the prophet on behalf of the people, which later (63:10ff.) turns into a lamenting petition (63:7—64:12). The whole section stresses Israel's dependence upon God. The date is sometime after the return from exile. All is far from well in the homeland, and the prayer becomes a plea for God's care. The verses of our passage, however, are words of thanksgiving for the Lord's acts of goodness in the past.

The prophet "recounts"—that is, he performs one of the most vital acts of Israel's religion by bringing into remembrance God's former "deeds of steadfast love." The Hebrew word for these deeds of unfailing love is *hesed* in the plural. It stands as both the first and last word of v. 7.

V. 8 recalls Exod. 19:5 and the language of covenant, and both v. 8 and v. 9 hark back to God's greatest act of salvation in Israel's history—the Exodus (cf. vv. 11-14). God had made Israel his people when he became their Deliverer or Savior.

The first words of v. 9 present translation problems. The RSV may offer a correct interpretation: "In all their affliction he was afflicted." It is more likely, however, that the other modern translations offer a better understanding by choosing to be led by the Septuagint Greek version: "He became their deliverer in all their troubles'' (NEB). In either case, the emphasis on the very presence of God himself would be a sufficient reason for the passage to be chosen as a lection for the Christmas season. Part of the miracle of the Exodus in Israel's remembrance was that it was God himself who performed this act and not an intermediary. It was through his love and his pity that he redeemed them.

Second Lesson: Gal. 4:4-7. The occasion for Paul's letter was the news that some of the Galatians had been persuaded that they had to take on certain parts of the Jewish law, including circumcision, if they were to be regarded as full disciples. "I am astonished," Paul writes (1:6); and he is also more than a little angry that his flock had so easily been led astray. Much of the letter is devoted to explaining to them how the relationship to God through law has been superseded by a relationship through faith in Christ. By way of analogy, Paul argues, individuals were formerly like small children, who, although they one day would come to their inheritance, were kept under guardianship and were little better than slaves. Then adding a new motif, Paul notes that those without Christ are also enslaved to the elemental spirits or powers, by which he may mean the strictures and precepts of human law, or he may mean the star-gods or fates, which are really no gods at all (cf. vv. 8-10). The two meanings are not necessarily exclusive.

Now, however, a new time has begun. God sent forth (*exapesteilen;* preexistence may be but need not be implied) his Son, who was born of a woman and was himself under the law. The argument assumes that the Son had to experience and to fulfill what he was to overcome. Note especially 3:13 where Christ undergoes the curse of the law.

Two results have been achieved (4:5). Christ's followers have been redeemed (that is, their freedom has been purchased as when a slave is manumitted; see also 3:13). More than this, not only are they no longer slaves, but they are "adopted" as sons, as the result of God's act in Christ.

The *hoti* which begins v. 6 may mean either "because you are sons" or "in order to show that you are sons." On one basis or the other, God has sent (*exapesteilen*) "the Spirit of his Son." Especially from the perspective of later Trinitarian reflection, this last phrase is fascinating. One might have expected the Spirit of God or the Holy Spirit. Is Paul thinking of the spirit by which Jesus lived and which enabled him to call upon God as his Father, or the divine Spirit which is of Christ as well as of God, or both?

This passage is paralleled by Rom. 8:14-23, verses which should be pondered for a fuller appreciation of Paul's meaning here. Unaided humanity could hardly be so bold as to presume to call upon the Almighty and All-Holy God of the universe as Father. But the Spirit comes into human hearts enabling this full access to God by those he has made his children. It is likely that the Aramaic *Abba* is reminiscent of Jesus' own use. It was a word which had special nuances of intimacy.

V. 7 sums the matter up: each disciple is no longer a slave to the law or the elemental spirits. Each has entered upon full maturity as a son and heir.

Gospel: John 1:1-18. The Fourth Gospel does not present either a human genealogy and birth narrative for Jesus or the story of his baptism. Instead this prologue establishes his eternal character in relationship to the Father and the divine origin of his mission. The verses introduce many of the major themes of the Gospel: witnessing, truth, life, Jesus' sonship, light which comes into the world of human affairs and is not overcome by darkness. This overture has the form of a poem into which prose parentheses seem to have been inserted.

The Greek imperfect tenses of the first verses stress the continuing being and relationship of the eternal Word with God. They are in contrast to the aorists in vv. 3, 6, and 14 which indicate the creative and historical activities of the Word. This "Word" (*logos*) has associations with both the divine reason (*logos* of Greek philosophy, the expressed form of God's thought) and the *memra* of late Jewish speculation (reaching back to the manner in which God spoke and it was so "in the beginning" of Gen. 1). It is anachronistic to ask about the precise nature of the relationship of Word and Father-God from the point of view of fourth- and fifth-century Christian doctrine. Here we are to understand that it is eternal and extraordinarily intimate. (With these verses one might also reflect on 1 John 1:1-3 and Heb. 1:1-3.)

Interesting textual problems and uncertainties with respect to punctuation affect the translation and meaning of vv. 3-4 and 18. The margins of the modern translations suggest the various possibilities for vv. 3-4. However it is read, the decisive role of the Word for all creation is clear. In v. 18 it cannot be determined whether we should read, "God, the only son," "the Son, the only one," or (less probably) "the only Son."

Along with the synoptics, the Fourth Gospel wishes to indicate the important place of John (the Baptizer) in the historical drama of salvation while yet refuting any suggestion that John himself was more than the one who witnessed to the true light. The verses referring to John seem like prose asides and are further developed in vv. 19–34.

While both Greek and Jewish speculative thought knew of an attribute or aspect of God known as Word or Wisdom, the astounding Christian claim is that this divine character entered directly and fully into human life. There seems to be a reference to this participation in v. 11, but it is made unmistakable in v. 14. The statement "the Word became flesh" was intended as a way of indicating this full participation. The "dwelling" (literally, "pitching a tent") of the Word among us and the beholding of God's "glory" are phrases rich with OT connotations. The direct revelation of the Word in the flesh of Jesus, however, fulfills and surpasses the Old Covenant. This is the grace (the Word) upon grace (the law) of v. 16. Even though "his own" (for the most part a reference to Judaism, but all humankind is in a sense included) did not accept the Word, those who have given Jesus, the Word incarnate, their trust are enabled to become God's children—not by natural birth (cf. 3:3–8) or by any physical process (v. 13) but by God's action.

HOMILETICAL INTERPRETATION

If you haven't already done so in going over the exegesis (above), read now (or reread!) the three texts that are before us. Read them aloud if possible, and compare several translations. Especially do not miss the sensitive, poetic rendering of John 1 in the New American Bible.

Most conspicuously, all three texts are celebrations of remembrance; all three recall from the past that which dramatically, decisively, categorically qualifies and transforms all that is subsequent to what is remembered. And all three insist that what is remembered is no accident of history, no result of the interaction of time and chance, nothing triggered by the effects of the "natural" process of cause and effect, nor yet by any kind of human manipulation. What is remembered is, quite simply, what God has done.

First Lesson: Isa. 63:7–9. In the two NT texts, Gal. 4:4–7 and John 1:1–18, it is the Christ Event that is celebrated, God's Event, transforming and redeeming all subsequent history in the life of faith. *In faith,* in Christian faith, it is the same essential, historically unified event that is held up in the brief text which is our First Lesson. Like the Word which was one with God from the beginning, the sustained redemptive action of God which the prophet remembers and celebrates in this passage is a unified whole, in all times and places. The people of God are redeemed in God's love and pity; and it is God's direct act! "It was not a messenger or an angel" but very God who saved them (see NAB and exegesis above).

It is sometimes remarked as curious that God is represented in the books of Isaiah and Ezekiel as insisting that God's redemptive act is for God's own sake and not on behalf of the redeemed. "For my name's sake I defer my anger. . . . Behold, I have refined you. . . . For my own sake, for my own sake, I do it" (Isa. 48:9–11 RSV, in part). And in Ezek. 36:22 ff. (RSV): "Thus says the Lord God: it is not for your sake, O house of Israel, that I am about to act [in your redemption], but for the sake of my holy name. . . . I will vindicate the holiness of my great name. . . . A new heart I will give you, and a new spirit I will put within you." The passage concludes in v. 32, "It is not for your sake that I will act, says the Lord God; let that be known to you."

Something of this sense is reflected in what immediately precedes our text, in Isaiah 63. The saving act was not of Israel's doing or, in-ferentially, by any human means: "my own arm brought me victory" over all that held you in bondage (v. 5).

The prophets in these passages appear to be hedging against the perennial tendency toward the assertion of human pride. What happens in human redemption is not by human merit, not by human initiative and effort, and certainly not by the pride of the redeemed. It is an act accomplished for God's sake: "in God's love and pity, he redeemed them" (v. 9); for, on account of, out of, God's own nature and purpose—in this sense, "for my own sake."

The prophetic hedge is against self-righteousness, self-deification, pride, to which humankind is always easily prey. Recall over recent years the times when, in effect, you have heard it said, we will redeem ourselves by our own creative genius: our science will save us (so one renowned Pulitzer Prize winner).

And yet there is a tender ambivalence in prophet and Gospel. Perhaps recalling Hosea's symbolic naming of one of his children "Not my people" (Hos. 1:9; cf. 2:23) and Isaiah's opening blast against "sons who deal corruptly" (Isa. 1:4), the prophet here in Isa. 63:8 hears God saying "for my own sake" not now harshly, but in profound compassion. "Surely they *are* my people, sons who will not deal falsely" (RSV, emphasis added).

The NT term *grace* embraces both the sense of "for my own sake" and "for your sake." Grace is precisely God's unmerited act of love and mercy; and since utterly unearned, it is for God's sake. But once received, the recipient cannot but say, in wonder and gratitude, "it is for me."

The closest Hebrew word is *ḥesed,* which opens and closes v. 7 (Isa. 63). There is no universally acceptable English rendering: "steadfast love" (RSV), "favors" and "great kindness" (NAB), "acts of unfailing love" and "acts of love" (NEB), "goodness" (JB), "unfailing love" and "constant love" (TEV).

When the prophet faces obduracy and arrogance and pride in the people of God, the Word, the corrective Word of redemption, is "for my own sake." But when the scene is one of sheep without a shepherd, the Word is the Word of compassion. The Word is *ḥesed* and grace.

Second Lesson: Gal. 4:4-7. These verses express the culmination of the sustained, unified, biblical event of human redemption. God sends his very Son, "born of a woman, born under the law," to change our status, to give us a new identity, to make of us new creatures in a new creation—no longer slaves to the master (the law), but children of God, the Holy Parent, and heirs of God, *by God's own act* (cf. NEB, Gal. 4:4-7).

Our annual celebration, commemoration, reenactment, reappropriation, of the culminating redemptive event serves to renew our mind and revive our consciousness of what has already occurred to transform us and our history, to clothe us in a new identity and to place us in a new creation. This is by God's own act, in a profound sense for God's own sake, but out of God's *ḥesed* and grace, which we have all received.

Gospel: John 1:1-18. Or, as the prologue to John's Gospel puts it (NAB):

> The Word became flesh
> and made his dwelling among us,
> and we have seen his glory:
> the glory of an only Son coming from the Father,
> filled with enduring love. . . .
>
> Of his fullness
> we have all had a share—
> love following upon love.

Finally, then, we have to say that love cannot be for its own sake—which is of course the problem in much that passes under the name of love in our own time. Love says nothing about the object of love except that it is loved; and it is in knowing the love of God in Christ that we are conscious recipients of *ḥesed* and grace.

In the mind of the biblically literate person, then and now, what is conjured up in that mind-blowing assertion that in Christ, the Word became flesh? Too much ever to be written down, of course; but it surely embraces the Word of justice, the setting right of what is wrong. It embraces the Word of creation, which always *is:* "Circumcision is nothing; uncircumcision is nothing; the only thing that counts is new creation!" (appropriately, among the closing words of Galatians—6:15 NEB). And the celebrative remembrance of the Word made flesh, the Christ Event, calls us back in the name of justice and new creation to the old, stubborn, obdurate, arrogant, prideful world waiting in poverty and oppression for the coming of Christ, the coming of justice and new creation.

Three texts insist that what is remembered is no accident of history. What is remembered is, quite simply, what God has done, what God is doing, and what God purposes to do in and through us, since

> Of his fullness
> we have all had a share—
> love following upon love.

The Name of Jesus (January 1)

Lutheran	Roman Catholic	Episcopal	Pres/UCC/Chr
Num. 6:22–27	Num. 6:22–27	Exod. 34:1–8	Deut. 8:1–10
Rom. 1:1–7 or Phil. 2:9–13	Gal. 4:4–7	Rom. 1:1–7 or Phil. 2:9–13	Rev. 21:1–7
Luke 2:21	Luke 2:16–21	Luke 2:15–21	Matt. 25:31–46

EXEGESIS

First Lesson: Deut. 8:1-10. One should be aware of at least two historical contexts while pondering these verses. The passage is part of one of several addresses or charges recorded in Deuteronomy as though they were delivered by Moses on the plains of Moab just before the people entered into the promised land. The understandings which most characterize this book, however, date from the reign of Josiah in Jerusalem—the period shortly before the Exile. A major theme is covenant renewal. The passage 8:1-10 is representative of a number of the book's urgent pleas to observe the Lord's statutes and to live in love, fidelity, and obedience to God. These passages are a kind of *anamnesis,* or remembering, which may at one time have had a liturgical context, and are intended to recall to the people their original covenant relationship. In the circumstances of Josiah's lifetime, Judah is seen to be in danger of allowing the customs and gods of foreign peoples to become their own, just as there had been a similar threat to Israel in the time of Moses (see chap. 7). If they follow other gods, they will suffer the fate of destruction and exile. But if they faithfully observe all that the Lord commands, they will know abundance and prosperity in the land which God gives them.

Deut. 8:1 sets forward this responsibility and promise quite clearly. The next verses then recall part of Israel's foundational experience—the hardships of the wilderness after the Exodus. They are interpreted here as discipline.

Of particular importance (v. 3) was the feeding with the manna. God who exacted this discipline also provided the means to endure it. The "man cannot live by bread alone" theme stresses the fullness of Israel's dependence on God, including both physical and spiritual sustenance. The statement is employed somewhat differently in the story of Jesus' temptation: Matt. 4:4; Luke 4:4. The collateral tradition of v. 4 is not found outside Deuteronomy.

V. 5 recognizes that discipline can be a sign of God's favor, perceiving that God can care for Israel as a father to a son. See Deut. 1:31 on God's fatherly care, and Prov. 3:12 with Heb. 12:5-6 on paternal discipline as an expression of this concern.

The description of the abundant land is a continuing motif (cf. 6:10-11; 8:12; 11:10-12) and stands in contrast to the deprivation of the wilderness. V. 9 is a kind of hyperbole, since there is little iron ore or bronze to be found in Palestine. V. 10 restates the reciprocity of this Covenant. As God has blessed Israel, so the people are to offer their blessing to God.

Second Lesson: Rev. 21:1-7. In the centuries before the birth of Christ there developed in Judaism a belief that human history would one day come to a final consummation bringing with it a great transformation, frequently pictured in terms of a glorious recreation. The author of Revelation was strongly influenced by this understanding, and his last chapters are interlaced with parallels and allusions to the dreams of OT prophetic hope.

This passage is also a culmination of the revelations given to John the Seer in which he foresaw myriad tribulations for the followers of Jesus. These were perceived to be governed by and reflective of a supernatural battle with God and his angels on one side and cosmic powers of evil on the other. Finally, all the forces of evil would be overcome, and after a universal judgment, the new world would commence. God is ultimately in charge of all history and, with his victorious Christ, will be triumphant over every form of evil.

V. 1 echoes Isa. 65:17; 66:22; 2 Cor. 5:17. See also Rom. 8:19–21. The passing away of the sea harks back to a creation myth in which the threatening chaotic waters were overcome by God. V. 2 indicates that the new creation will appear not in heaven itself but will come from heaven to a transformed world. Fulfilling Israel's dreams, it will be a glorious new Jerusalem, contrasting sharply with the corrupt and defeated Babylon of chaps. 14—18. The image of the redeemed community as the Lord's bride is familiar in Scripture. See Jer. 2:2; Hos. 2:14, 16. Compare 2 Cor. 11:2; Eph. 5:25–33; Rev. 19:7, which depict the church as the bride of *Christ*.

The theme in v. 3 of God dwelling in intimate relation with his people (or quite possibly peoples, conveying a more universalistic note) again fulfills OT dreams: Lev. 26:11–12; Ezek. 37:26–28. The thought is given its special Christian meaning in John 1:14.

On the wiping away of tears and the end of mourning, cf. Isa. 25:8; 35:10; Rev. 7:17. On the overcoming of death, see Isa. 25:8 and 1 Cor. 15:54. For significant cross-references to God's bold declaration of v. 5, see above on v. 1.

God is earlier described as the Alpha and Omega (the first and last letters of the Greek alphabet) in 1:8 as is Jesus in 22:13. (Cf. 1:17; Isa. 44:6; 48:12.) The water from the fountain of life calls to mind the river flowing from Eden in Genesis. In the often parched land of Palestine, water was a forceful symbol of life-giving power. See Isa. 55:1, where it is also without price, as it is in Rev. 22:17 as well.

The "he who conquers" of v. 7 recalls the same expression used repeatedly to encourage Christian witness in chaps. 2—3. The resulting sonship is reminiscent of the motif of Israel as God's son in the OT and also of the messianic references in Pss. 2:7; 89:27–28. More significantly still, one thinks of the heritage of sonship which Christians experience through the activity of the Spirit as described in Rom. 8:15-17; Gal. 4:6-7.

Gospel: Matt. 25:31-46. The parable comes at the conclusion of Matthew's version of Jesus' last discourse with his followers. The words parallel and reinforce one of the Gospel's vital themes: decisions made and actions done now determine one's destiny in the age to come. While this imaginative scene is found only in Matthew, and displays a number of signs of the evangelist's particular interests, many scholars believe that its central message reaches back to Jesus. In its entirety the passage is a mixture of forms: a basic simile about the separation of sheep and goats (compare other probably authentic parables of Jesus regarding the wheat and weeds and good and bad fish) followed by a series of sayings. The evangelist may well have supplied the apocalyptic frame and details which add to the whole an allegorical coloring.

Matthew's Gospel gives special emphasis to Jesus as the Son of man at the time of eschatological judgment. Nor could many readers of this Gospel forget that it was Jesus as the Son of man who had nowhere to lay his head (8:20), who was rejected and put to death. In this sense he too was one of the "least ones" (vv. 40, 45).

The evangelist may well have inserted the designations King and Lord (intending them to refer to Jesus as Son of man), along with the conception of the eternal messianic kingdom in v. 34. His hand may also be seen in the plural "nations" (v. 32), which lends a universalistic tone.

The imagery of the separation of sheep from goats was a familiar one, the darker-colored goats being herded away at night to protect them from the cold against which they had less defence. Hearers of Jesus' parable may have recalled Ezek. 34:17ff., although there the final separation is between fat and lean sheep.

Did the evangelist (and perhaps Jesus before him) intend to focus the care and charity which were to form the basis of judgment *within* the circle of Christian disciples? Quite possibly so. "Brothers" (v. 40), although it may be a Matthean addition, refers in this Gospel only to Jesus' followers. It is likely that the understanding of the story originally depended on the awareness of the principle according to which the acceptance or rejection of a person's agent was tantamount to rejection or acceptance of the sender. In this light only Jesus' disciples would be seen as his agents, and one must compare Mark 9:41 = Matt. 10:42 in this regard.

In the context of the entire NT and the developing Christian mission, however, the story breaks out of any narrow definitions. While such charitable behavior on the part of Christians may, and perhaps in some sense must, begin within the Christian community, the heart of Jesus' teaching militates against any legalism which would confine it within this circle. In this light the parable may be read as a creative response by the church to the absence of their Lord while they awaited his Parousia: he may be loved in those who represent him in the world. *In the end,* that group will be seen to include all those who are in need.

HOMILETICAL INTERPRETATION

The three texts, Deut. 8:1-10, Rev. 21:1-7, and Matt. 25:31-46, may be called utopian, if one stretches the term in the case of the third. In Deuteronomy the sense is clearly that you can have it now—just do what we tell you and all will be well. In Revelation God with a victorious Christ will marvelously effect not only a new earth but a new heaven as well, and the state of humankind will be one of bliss. In Matthew a powerful case is made that what one does about the miserable of the earth determines one's ultimate and presumably everlasting existence in "the kingdom prepared for you from the foundations of the world" (v. 34 RSV) or in "the eternal fire prepared for the devil and his angels" (v. 41 RSV). Those who live now in indifference and neglect toward the marginalized and victimized of the earth "will go away into eternal punishment," while those who live for the impoverished, the alienated, the lonely, the wretched—those who, even without knowing it, make identity with the powerless and the anguished—"will go away . . . into eternal life" (v. 46 RSV).

First Lesson: Deut. 8:1-10. The two NT texts look for consummation beyond present existence, one to a divinely transformed age, the other to eternal life beyond present temporal experience. Deuteronomy—not simply in the text before us but in the entire book—sees reality in terms of this life and understands that total fulfillment is, quite simply, Yahweh's reward for faithful obedience of (Deuteronomic) law. The law is delivered by Moses. This is the setting of Deuteronomy, although we have every reason to think that this book received its present formulation in the seventh century B.C. and was the basis for elaborate and thorough reform of religious practice in Jerusalem and Judah (the southern kingdom) in the midst of the reign of the good King Josiah around 621 (see the account of this in 2 Kings

22—23). The repeated sense of Deuteronomy is that obedience to the law will surely result in a long, rich, and contented life in the land, the lovely land, which is itself the gift of Yahweh. It is "a land in which you will eat bread without scarcity, in which you will lack nothing" (v. 9 RSV). Against the protest to this simple scheme of obedience and reward which inevitably arose from inevitable contrary experience, the text suggests, on the basis of crises of hunger in the wilderness experience, that Yahweh means to teach his people that they do not live by bread alone, but by all that proceeds from the mouth of Yahweh— that is, that it is the Word that in the last analysis sustains the life of the people (see v. 3).

Now we know, as certainly did also the ancient scribes of the law, that in reality loyalty to the ways and will of God does not necessarily issue in a long and fulfilled life. The good and the just and the compassionate are by no means exempt from the slings and arrows of outrageous fortune, as one of the most brilliant writings of the OT, Job, is conceived and fashioned to say. But, as also must have been the case among the faithful in Josiah's time, we have no difficulty in translating terms of benign physical and temporal blessing to the totality of the blessing of heart and mind and soul and strength that is the gift of commitment to God in Jesus Christ. And *of course* we affirm with our text that we do not indeed live toward and by and for the exclusively physical satisfactions ("bread alone"), but by the Word (that which "proceeds out of the mouth of Yahweh"), and especially the Word made flesh in Jesus Christ, as so recently we celebrated (see Matt. 4:4 and Luke 4:4).

Second Lesson: Rev. 21:1-7. A new heaven and a new earth—'tis a consummation devoutly to be wished! I remember still the young man in a novel of some years back, who, setting forth on what was to be a strange and remarkable adventure, said that he did not know where he was going, but that he was quite sure about what he needed —a new land, a new race, a new language, and a new mystery.

This is the perennial word for the new year. Of course we will not find the literal new heaven and new earth any more than we will be given in return for faithfulness the life of physical and material bliss. But we will purpose anew to appropriate anew the qualities that ensue from commitment, that inhere in the promise that in very truth all things are made new in the Word of God (Rev. 21:5), that chaos cannot anymore engulf us ("the sea was no more," v. 1; see exegesis above), and that in reality newness of life is ours since (v. 3) God's home is with us!

You may want to recall the persistence of the theme of the new creation in the OT, and especially the rhapsodic sounding of the theme in the latter chapters of Isaiah—42:7-10; 43:19; 48:6; 62:2; 65:17; 66:22. Try a reading that puts these in all but ecstatic coherence. Add Jer. 31:22; 31:31; Lam. 3:23; Ezek. 11:19; 18:31; 36:26. What better for January one!

Gospel: Matt. 25:31-46. It would be difficult to find anything in the Bible more powerful (and in certain senses, more devastating) than this story of the last judgment in Matthew 25; and I underscore Dean Borsch's reminder, above, that "many scholars believe that its central message reaches back to Jesus."

In connection with all the lessons covered in this volume, I commend to your reading a book written by Robert McAfee Brown, *Theology in a New Key* (Philadelphia: Westminster Press, 1978). It is a fine review of liberation theology (so-called), with both pros and cons. It contains a brief section on Matthew 25 (pp. 95-97):

> One thing usually overlooked is that the judgment rendered is not against individuals but against nations: "Before him will be gathered *all the nations.*" The familiar obligations to feed the hungry, visit the sick, and clothe the naked are not merely requirements of private, individualistic ethics; they are demands made upon the *social* structures of which we are a part. This is a terrifying prospect for a nation like ours which . . . has 6 percent of the world's population and consumes 40 percent of the world's resources.

> This social dimension of judgment is crucial, but it must not be used to let individuals off the hook. For both nations and individuals the story tells us that the ultimate test, the criterion of final accountability in God's sight, is *not* Do you know the creed, do you pray, are you careful about Sabbath observance, do you mention God in your constitution and on your coins? but rather, *What did you do for those in need?* The test is not "knowing" but "doing," or rather, it is recognizing that the only true knowing [of God] comes by doing.

I rather suspect that most of us in the family of readers of Proclamation 2 do not subscribe to any literalist views of eternal punishment (Matt. 25:46). But it is important to acknowledge what is implicit in this statement, namely, the overwhelming indictment of those who choose to go their own way, insensitive, indifferent, and therefore self-serving.

January one. Deuteronomy 8 summons us, with promise of ultimate gratification, to renewed obedience to what we know the will of God to be; and it reminds us in the midst of our own constant temptation to live by and for bread alone, that it is only the Word of God by which we are sustained and renewed. V. 3 is quoted in the story of Jesus' temptation in Matt. 4:4 and Luke 4:4.

January one. The word of Rev. 21:1-7 may be linked with Paul's near-closing line in Galatians (6:15) which we have already quoted in connection with the First Sunday after Christmas above: "Circumcision is nothing; uncircumcision is nothing; the only thing that counts is *new creation!*" (NEB, emphasis added).

January one. The story of the last judgment in Matthew 25 tells us that the whole enterprise, human and divine, is lost if *we* are not actively a part of the creation of a new heaven and a new earth.

And the sum of it, following hard upon our celebration of the gift of God in Christ, is simply and adequately and redemptively that God's home is with the human family (Rev. 21:3).

The Second Sunday after Christmas

Lutheran	Roman Catholic	Episcopal	Pres/UCC/Chr	Meth/COCU
Isa. 61:10— 62:3	Sir. 24:1-4, 8-12	Jer. 31:7-14	Prov. 8:22-31	Isa. 61:10— 62:3 or Sir. 24:1-2, 8-12
Eph. 1:3-6, 15-18	Eph. 1:3-6, 15-18	Eph. 1:3-6, 15-19a	Eph. 1:15-23	Eph. 1:3-6, 15-23
John 1:1-18	John 1:1-18 or John 1:1-5, 9-14	Matt. 2:13-15, 19-23 or Luke 2:41-52 or Matt. 2:1-12	John 1:1-5, 9-14	Matt. 2:13-15, 19-23

EXEGESIS

First Lesson: Sir. 24:1-4, 8-12. The Wisdom of Jesus the Son of Sirach, often known simply as Sirach, and later called Ecclesiasticus (or "church book"), was originally composed about 180 B.C. by a Jewish wisdom teacher. It stands in a long line of proverbial teaching in Judaism. Our passage is a hymn in praise of Wisdom, placed between long sections of practical and prudential counsel. It is meant to help interpret and provide a larger perspective for the proverbial teachings, since they are all understood to be inspired by the divine Wisdom.

In the centuries before the birth of Christ, this Wisdom came to be appreciated as more than an attribute of God. She was spoken of as a personification of a divine activity. At least in certain circles Wisdom was regarded as a kind of emanation from God which acted for him especially in the creation of the world and in the giving of understanding and the knowledge of God's ways to humanity. Compare particularly Prov. 8:22-36 on which Sirach 24 is in part modeled. In her creative work Wisdom was often closely linked with the related conceptions of the Spirit of God which moved over the waters (Gen. 1:2) and the words or Word of God which he spoke in order to make all things (Gen. 1). Cf. also Ps. 33:6; Isa. 55:11. Wisdom—cosmic in nature, yet coming to dwell amid human life; ultimately related to God, yet in some measure distinct—understandably came to be regarded by Christians as a prefiguration of Jesus as the creative Word of God become incarnate (John 1:1-4). Hence the selection of this reading during the Christmas season.

Wisdom is said to speak her own praises among her people (that is, Israel, anticipating v. 8) and before the divine council which ministers before God (cf. Pss. 82:1; 89:5-7). The two opening verses succinctly indicate that Wisdom is at home in both the natural and supernatural realms.

The mist of v. 3 alludes to the mist described in Gen. 2:6 in the second of the creation stories. It is a kind of parallel for the creative wind or Spirit of God in Gen. 1:2. V. 4 pictures a throne in the heights of heaven above the vault of the sky. The author is most likely thinking of the pillar of cloud as the symbol of the Lord's presence in the Sinai desert. See Exod. 13:21-22; 33:9. Here and in vv. 5-6, Wisdom is portrayed as both cosmic and yet present everywhere in the world.

Vv. 8-12 tell of Wisdom's particular assignment by God to dwell with the people of Israel. There is a particular focus on Wisdom's role in the worship of God, both in the desert tabernacle (see again Exod. 33:9-10) and in the temple at Jerusalem. V. 12 echoes the language of Deut. 32:9.

Second Lesson: Eph. 1:3-6, 15-18. The Letter to the Ephesians is traditionally regarded as an epistle of Paul written during a period of imprisonment (possibly at the same time as Colossians, with which it has many affinities), perhaps in Rome in the early 60s. A number of scholars believe, however, that the letter was actually composed a generation or so later, being intended as a kind of recapitulation of the apostle's thought and a way of setting forth what he would have said were he alive at that time. The verses chosen for our lection are part of a lengthy opening hymn of praise and thanksgiving (vv. 3–14) which then is transposed to a tone of intercession mixed with gratitude in vv. 15–18. It is an outpouring of praise, probably based on liturgical language which was used in association with baptism. The motifs of bestowal of spiritual blessing, election, dedication, and sonship would certainly belong in such a setting, and the character of the intercessions seems to fit. The major concerns of the letter are to place the salvation wrought by God in Christ in the context of a universal perspective of salvation history, and to show how this act of God has effected both a new cosmic unity and the unity of Jews and Gentiles in a saved humanity. The opening verses are also especially concerned to stress the belief that all this is no accident of history but rather part of God's plan determined in heaven before the creation.

The expression in v. 3 "in Christ" (or its equivalent) is used with great frequency in Ephesians and suggests a form of incorporation of the Christian into the new life of Christ and his body, the church. The spiritual blessings (that is, blessings given through the Spirit) are described below. They are in "the heavenly places"; that is, they originate from a realm above all human uncertainties and vicissitudes. The author's interest in v. 4 is to confirm the certainty of God's eternal purposes rather than the predestination of individuals. The language is reminiscent of God's calling of Israel. "Without blemish" recalls the requirements for OT sacrifice. In v. 5 the underlying Greek expression means "to be adopted as sons." It stresses God's initiative. The references to God's pleasure (v. 5) and to Christ as the Beloved (v. 6) call to mind Jesus' own baptism. See Mark 1:11.

V. 15 does sound a somewhat strange note if Paul himself is actually writing to the Ephesians, since he had lived there for three years. Whoever the author, he now offers his unceasing prayer that these chosen ones may have the gifts of wisdom and vision befitting their election (cf. Col. 1:9; 2 Thess. 1:11). This wisdom is a revelation of the Spirit, bringing knowledge of God's universal plan of salvation (on which cf. 1:9–10 and the comments above). Such insight into the hope and rich heritage of God's people, the new Israel, is given inwardly—through 'the eyes of the heart'; that is, the human mind illumined by God.

Gospel: Matt. 2:13-15, 19-23. The evangelist's major purposes in the nativity stories were to show that from his birth Jesus was the Chosen One of God, the Messiah of Israel, and that all that happened was not a series of accidents in human history but part of God's plan. All takes place in fulfillment of the prophecies of the sacred Scriptures of Judaism. The story of the visit of the magi (2:1-12) introduces the realization that this child is also destined to be the Savior for gentile peoples. The continuation of the narrative in the passages which form our lection is used to reinforce the belief in scriptural fulfillment and typology and correspondingly to explain why it was that Jesus came to live in Galilee rather than Bethlehem, the town of Messiah's birth. Since there are no other Christian or non-Christian parallels to these materials, many historians have come to regard them as legends told to establish the evangelist's theological understandings. Above all they illustrate that God was at work in the life of Jesus of Nazareth to carry out his design of salvation.

The account of the withdrawal into Egypt and the return is told with a remarkable economy of detail. At 2:13, as at other critical junctures in the infancy narratives, the action is guided by a dream. Joseph is once again the recipient. See 2:19 and 1:20, where also an angel conveys the message. In what follows the evangelist consciously uses typology. As ancient Israel had its form of exile in Egypt, so did Jesus. A parallel is being drawn with Joseph going down to Egypt. Then Jesus, too, is called out of Egypt to return to the land of Israel. This is a second Exodus, helping Christians to understand that through Jesus a new drama of salvation is begun. Their Lord and his followers have become the new Israel. Using a formula with which he often introduces OT texts, Matthew quotes Hos. 11:1. This neatly adds the thought that Jesus is now God's special son as Israel had earlier been chosen for that particular and intimate relationship with God.

Moses, too, had been persecuted by a king as a baby. He also had been hidden in order to be saved. Here, and elsewhere in his Gospel, Matthew perceives Jesus to be the one who had been promised to succeed Moses. The measure of the consciousness of this parallelism in the evangelist's mind is disclosed in 2:20, where the verbal similarity with Exod. 4:19 is striking. Moses can return to his ministry in Egypt because "the men who were seeking your life are dead." The parallel accounts for the plural in Matthew's phrasing.

These parallels, of course, are only approximate, and we today are likely to find them a less useful mode of argument. But they were an important form of reasoning in Matthew's time and helped to establish the conviction, which we can share, that God's purposes were being fulfilled even in the most obscure human circumstances.

Finally, Matthew stretches this method to account for the fact that

Jesus was raised in the little Galilean hamlet of Nazareth (a town unknown in the OT or later Jewish writings) and that Jesus came to be referred to as Jesus of Nazareth, or the Nazarene or Nazorean. What exactly was in the evangelist's mind is unclear. There is no obvious OT reference to support the prediction that he should be called a Nazarene. Perhaps this is why Matthew refers rather generally to the prophets in the plural. One possibility is that the derivation is from *nāzir* and the ancient Israelite Nazirite vow through which a child was dedicated to God and an ascetic style of life. See Num. 6:1-21; Judg. 13:2-7; 1 Sam. 1:11; and of John Baptist, Luke 1:15. Alternatively it is felt that the evangelist had in mind the similarity of sound with the *netzer* in Isa. 11:1. Jesus was the "branch" from the roots of Jesse, David's father.

HOMILETICAL INTERPRETATION

The "middle" text, Eph. 1:3-6, 15-18, ties together the first and third, the reading from Sirach (Ecclesiasticus) 24:1-4, 8-12, and the Gospel passage in Matt. 2:13-15, 19-23.

The first, one of the great classical descriptions of Wisdom, is instructive to the third. We have already looked at the identification of Christ with Wisdom in a preceding discussion; and although the term Wisdom does not occur in our Gospel, to understand it as implicit there enhances the story of the flight into Egypt, the Egyptian sojourn, and the return to Nazareth. This story tells how the Word, which is Wisdom, which is Christ, "took root among the people whom the Lord had honoured by choosing them to be his special possession" (Sir. 24:12 NEB).

Ephesians puts a bridge between the two. "May the God of our Lord Jesus Christ . . . grant you a spirit of wisdom and insight to know him clearly" (1:17 NAB).

First Lesson: Sir. 24:1-4, 8-12. If you choose to make this Sunday an occasion on which to preach on Christ as Wisdom, you will want to review the greatest OT Wisdom texts, Proverbs 8 and Job 28; perhaps some of the wisdom psalms (especially 1, 37, 49, 73, 112, 128); and like Sirach, an apocryphal writing, the Wisdom of Solomon—especially chap. 8.

It is well to remember that ancient Israel's religious leadership was of three major types, set forth explicitly in the words of Jer. 18:18: ". . . . the *law* shall not perish from the priest, nor *counsel* from the wise, nor the *word* from the prophet'' (RSV, emphasis added). In meaningful ways all three—law, counsel, and word—are met in Christ.

We have earlier considered the influence of the Wisdom concept on the prologue to the Fourth Gospel in John 1. The Greek term for "Word" embraces the classical concept of Wisdom. It was in the beginning with God and was a participant in all that was made. Similarly, as the exegesis points out above, Sir. 24:3 affirms Wisdom's existence before anything was: "it was I who covered the earth like a mist" (NEB)—an unmistakable reference to Gen. 2:5-6. Before there were shrubs and plants and people on the earth, "a mist went up from the earth and watered the whole face of the ground" (RSV). The one who comes, like Moses and indeed the whole ancient Israelite people, out of totally unprepossessing and even improbable beginnings, and survives all the hazards that inhere in the lines "into Egypt" and "out of Egypt" again (see exegesis above), this one, this One, this Word, this Wisdom, already was even before the beginning! It is this realization that certainly in part provokes the magnificent poem of Philippians 2 (TEV):

He always [!] had the nature of God,
   but he did not think that by force he should try to become equal with God.
Instead of this, of his own free will he gave up all he had,
   and took the nature of a servant.
. . . .
and appeared in human likeness.

"Wisdom is at home in both the natural and supernatural realms. . . . Wisdom is portrayed as both cosmic and yet present everywhere in the world" (exegesis above). So it was consistently with the ancient notion of Wisdom. So it was with Christ-as-Wisdom in John 1. So in Philippians 2. So, of course, in incarnation. And so it was, too, in the prophetic understanding: the Holy One *in your midst* (Hos. 11:9). Natural and supernatural, cosmic and present, the Word of the prophet and the Wisdom of the sage are nowhere more effectively united than in Isa. 57:15 (RSV):

For thus says the high and lofty One
   who inhabits eternity, whose name is Holy:
I dwell in the high and holy place,
   and also with [anyone] who is of a contrite and humble spirit,
to revive the spirit of the humble,
   and to revive the heart of the contrite.

Compare this passage with the lesson from Sirach: "The Creator of the universe laid a command upon me; / my Creator decreed where I should dwell. / He said, 'Make your home in Jacob; / find your heritage in Israel.' / Before time began [God] created me, / and I shall remain for ever" (Sir. 24:8-9 NEB).

The Wisdom concept adds significantly, profoundly, to the understanding of the Christ Event.

Second Lesson: Eph. 1:3-6, 15-18. "Blessed be God . . . who has blessed us with all the spiritual blessings of heaven in Christ" (*recall that Christ has been identified as the Cosmic and the Present, the Holy One in our midst, the Word and the Wisdom of God*). "Before the world was made, [God] chose us, chose us in Christ" (*recall that Christ is both Word and Wisdom, which were in the beginning with God*) ". . . for [God's] own kind purposes" (Eph. 1:3-6 JB).

This is the post-Event assessment of the gift of God in Christ; and the depth and magnitude and meaning of the gift can begin to be comprehended only in the light of the law (instruction) of the OT priest, the wisdom of the sage, and the word of the prophet (see Jer. 18:18, quoted above). The passage here is probably set in the form of a liturgy of the early Christian community.

I shall never forget wrestling with the question of authorship of Ephesians in a small seminary class. One day we would say, "It must be Paul"; and the next, "It can't be." Paul must have had his disciples as Isaiah did. And whether we are dealing with Paul or a disciple, what is sure is that we are coming here into the life and faith of the early church. Its prayer is (or ought to be, then and now) that God may give us the spiritual powers of Wisdom and vision by which comes knowledge of him (God, Christ, or God-in-Christ). That is NEB. Or, God grant us a spirit of Wisdom and insight to know him clearly (NAB). One thinks of the line in the song 'Day by Day' from Godspell. Again, God give us a spirit of Wisdom and perception of what is revealed, to bring us to full knowledge of him (JB). I have made bold to capitalize Wisdom because it seems improbable that the term can be employed here without connotations of the classical formulation of Wisdom.

In the lectionary selection of the three texts for the Second Sunday after Christmas, the passage from Ephesians provides for the church's appropriation of the ancient concept of Wisdom and its realization in the incarnation of Wisdom and Word (and law as well—Matt. 5:17) in Jesus Christ.

Gospel: Matt. 2:13-15, 19-23. In the exegesis, hard historical questions are rightly raised about the absolute "facticity" of Matthew 2, the flight of Joseph and Mary with the infant Jesus into Egypt, and their return to Nazareth after Herod's death. Matthew, more than either of the other synoptic writers, Mark or Luke, is eager to see in the OT the foreshadowing of events in the Christ story. It is the Word of God through the prophet Hosea that "out of Egypt I called my son" (11:1). Hosea, of course, meant the people of ancient Israel who went into Egypt and out again in the latter half of the second millennium B.C. But this Christ is *the* Son of God; and the experience of the OT people (and Moses their leader) prefigured what was (must have been) the story of the incarnate Christ. So, too, the return to Nazareth in fulfillment of the prophecy "He will be called a Nazarene." This one bristles with problems, which the exegesis reviewed.

Aristotle's distinction between historian and poet may be applicable to our understanding and affirmation of the Gospel. Aristotle's historian was a mere chronicler of sequential events; his poet was one who distilled from the chronological catalog its essence, its universal judgment, and its meaning. The synoptic writers were poet-historians, consumingly interested not in the chronological catalog but in the meaning of the Christ Event; and we who read them know and understand that fact and truth are not coextensive, that truth in meaning can be transcendent of fact. Wisdom and Word invest the Christ Event with its true meaning, meaning in truth; and Matthew's "typological" reading of OT story and word underscores what is not necessarily in the realm of "facticity" but what is, in faith, profoundly true. This event of the incarnation of Wisdom and Word in Christ is that consummation toward which all the history of God and his people in the OT was pointing and moving.

An artist like our poet-historian breaks up the world of fact by making us see comparisons, analogies, meanings that we never saw before. Such things lead to nothing, of course, except our own deeper understanding of ourselves and of the rest of humanity—and in this case, of the event of God's coming to dwell in our midst in Jesus Christ.